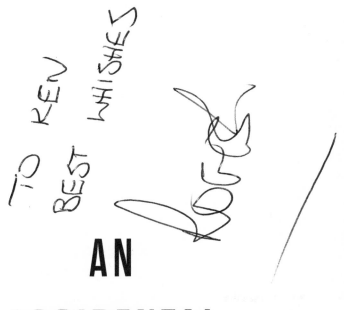

TO KEN
BEST WISHES

AN
ACCIDENTAL
HUMANITARIAN

A Memoir

ROGER JOHN FOWLER

 FriesenPress

One Printers Way
Altona, MB R0G 0B0
Canada

www.friesenpress.com

ISBN
978-1-03-913018-0 (Hardcover)
978-1-03-913017-3 (Paperback)
978-1-03-913019-7 (eBook)

1. BIOGRAPHY & AUTOBIOGRAPHY, PERSONAL MEMOIRS

Distributed to the trade by The Ingram Book Company

for Sara

Praise for *An Accidental Humanitarian*

At once a love story; powerful day-to-day insights into the work of an International Red Cross delegate; and horrific accounting of the war crimes of 1992-1996 Bosnia, *An Accidental Humanitarian* tells an anything but accidental story. Roger Fowler's story of service is deeply compelling. I couldn't put it down.

> — Lorimer Shenher, author of *That Lonely Section of Hell: The Botched Investigation of a Serial Killer Who Almost Got Away* and *This One Looks Like a Boy: My Gender Journey to Life as a Man*

This is a must read for anyone interested in the realities of delivering humanitarian aid under war time conditions. This timely reminder of the challenges, though set in the aftermath of the collapse of Yugoslavia, has important lessons for those now engaged in the delivery of humanitarian aid in war torn Ukraine.

> — Samuel Schwisberg, Former General Counsel, Canadian Red Cross Society and author of *Swarm Before Me: The Tragic Case of Becker V Pettkus*

Roger Fowler's memoir takes us into the operational heart of a terrible recent conflict. His personal observations are more relevant than ever, in the light of Russia's horrific attack on Ukraine.

> — Lynne Van Luven, Editor and former journalist

*Dedicated to all the thin, displaced, misplaced,
lost and tumbled, reluctant vagabonds.*

Table of Contents

* * * * *

I see their pain, their hurt
Suffering
I stand in awe
Amidst the ruins
Smoke and noise
Crashing sounds
This brutal war
It knows no bounds

I'll share your wounds
And keep them true
Deep
Silent
The smoke is gone
Just noise remains

I'll go home soon

~ RJF 1995

Becoming A Humanitarian

* * * * *

Thursday, September 8, 1994, just outside the Bihać Pocket

It was perfectly made and perfectly painted, so full of sadness, that tiny white coffin. I had first spotted it two days before, tucked away in a quiet corner where the mail destined for the sub-delegations was kept. I hoped I would not be tasked with its delivery, but here it was on the floor of my Land Cruiser, being tossed around with all the other equipment: shovel, blankets, wheel jack, snow chains, tools, spare parts, extra fuel, medical kit, sleeping bag, stove and water. With Bob Dylan playing "Blowin' in the Wind", I edged off the road onto a section of dried-out riverbed. I had used the route many times since arriving in the former Yugoslavia.

Suddenly, the Army of the Republika Srpska Krajina started firing OGANJ 128-millimetre multiple rockets over my head. As usual, I had forgotten my flak jacket and helmet; feeling exposed, I sped up, hearing the little coffin bouncing around. Realizing the rockets were not aimed at me but into the town, I eased off and took a breath. *What am I doing here?*

* * *

Operation Storm was the largest battle on European soil since the Second World War. The last major battle of the Croatian War of Independence, the operation covered 10,400 square kilometres across a front of 628 kilometres. Between dawn on August 4 to the evening of August 8, 1995, when the operation was declared over, 200,000 civilians were displaced. Most sources agree that during and in the days following the end of Operation Storm, 1,192 Serbian civilians were murdered or missing. And I cannot forget the nine elderly Serbs senselessly killed as an apparent act of vengeance in the village of Varivode, in the municipality of Knin on September 28, 1995, *six* weeks after the battle ended. During the entire bitter conflict in the former Yugoslavia, Croatian civilians suffered equally; other ethnic groups were harrowed by rape and murder as well.

* * *

This memoir is about my experiences during the nearly two years I worked with the largest humanitarian organization in the world, the International Committee of the Red Cross, during the war in the former Yugoslavia. The history of the Balkans is deep and complicated. I take responsibility for any errors I have made regarding dates, places and times. I have changed the names of individuals to observe confidentiality.

One of the last acts of hostility of the siege occurred at around 6 p.m. on January 9, 1996, when a single rocket-propelled grenade was fired at a tram running down the main street of Sarajevo, killing a 55-year-old woman, Mirsada Durić, and wounding 19 others[1].

What was I doing here? I came for the adventure and excitement only a war could provide. Or so I thought.

---

1   Wikipedia, s.v. "Siege of Sarajevo," last modified September 17, 2021, at 06:37 (UTC). https://en.wikipedia.org/wiki/Siege_of_Sarajevo

CHAPTER 1

The Cotswolds

* * * * *

On a typically wet and windy late January day, high in the Cotswolds in the southwest of England, my friend and workmate Andy and I were converting a large seventeenth-century stone barn into a house. As we measured and hammered, we discussed the nightly BBC news broadcast. It seemed there was an outrage exacted every day in the war in the former Yugoslavia, a place I could drive to in just twenty-four hours. Andy mentioned that the British Red Cross (BRC) were recruiting heavy-goods truck drivers to deliver humanitarian relief supplies in the conflict zone. I had never considered myself a humanitarian, but the work sounded interesting. The fact that the recruitment required working in an active conflict zone didn't particularly bother me. I have always believed, if you find yourself in a tough spot, you get yourself out of it. Over the next twenty months, that casual point of view would change.

After lunch, the rain was still coming down – not enough to call a halt to work but enough for me to put on my second work jacket. I have a two-jacket rule: as soon as one jacket is soaked through, change it for the second; when that starts to leak, it's time to go home or to the pub.

During the mid-seventies, I'd had numerous adventures driving heavy-goods trucks – semis – across Europe into the Eastern Bloc countries of Czechoslovakia, Hungary, Romania, Bulgaria and Yugoslavia. Also, I had driven across the Middle Eastern countries of Turkey, Iraq, Saudi Arabia, Jordan, Syria and Lebanon. So, I had solid experience as a truck driver in the former Yugoslavia and surrounding countries. Working in the fine drizzle that afternoon, as I relived some of those experiences, the appeal of another adventure drew me in. At forty, I was at a loss regarding my immediate future. My marriage had recently broken down and although I would miss my two adolescent boys terribly, I figured that I wouldn't be far away, just in southern Europe really, and I wouldn't be gone long.

That evening I asked one of my sisters to type my resume and a cover letter explaining to the BRC my interest in working for them. Five days later, with the rain coming down in sheets, they called and asked if I would come to their Hyde Park offices in London for an interview. The call caught me by surprise as I'd thought that my application would be filed along with others and forgotten. The meeting was two days away; that would give me enough time to get my story straight. The hour-long interview was relaxed and friendly; they said they would let me know. I thought straight away, *That means no.*

Off home I went, feeling a bit confused. I thought I did pretty well with the questions. *But never mind. They reimbursed me for a cheese and tomato sandwich and the train fare to the interview.* And it had been a nice change to get out of the rain on the job site. *Really,* I semi-convinced myself, *I don't want to go to Yugoslavia anyway!*

To my absolute delight, two days later, the BRC called to ask if I would go back to Hyde Park the following week for a two-day induction course. I was thinking, *This must mean I have the job, provided I do well on the course!*

February 5, 1994: British aid driver 'was shot in back of head'.

Paul Goodall, 35, was shot three times in the head after gunmen hijacked the Land Rover he was driving in Zenica, a Muslim controlled area of Central Bosnia. Two aid workers with him were wounded but escaped[2].

Zenica, Bosnia, 1994

2   https://www.independent.co.uk/news/uk/british-aid-driver-was-shot-in-back-of-head-1391994.html

Hearing this brought home to me that there really was a war going on.

Family and friends asked me if I was still going. My answer was, "Yes."

The following week, after two thorough and intense days, including a full medical examination, I proudly clutched a piece of paper that said I "was for immediate overseas deployment." I walked out of the BRC offices checked, inspected, injected, briefed, cleared and ready to go to war.

The Overseas Personnel Officer directed me to go to the Land Rover plant in Coventry where four other drivers and I were to collect an armoured Land Rover each and drive to Zagreb, the capital of Croatia. When we arrived, we were to report to the International Committee of the Red Cross (ICRC) offices. The ICRC would then take over responsibility for us during our six-month mission as truck drivers delivering humanitarian relief. The overseas officer explained that the ICRC was a Swiss humanitarian organization based in Geneva, and that they recruited non-Swiss personnel through National Red Cross Societies, including the BRC. She said the ICRC were active only in areas of conflict, and I would be working alongside many other National Society staff, including those from the Netherlands, Germany and Iceland. In fact, any National Society that had a budget to support their Red Cross personnel might be deployed to a mission. I didn't understand too much of the complexity of the international organization, but the Land Rovers sounded like fun.

Friday, February 11, 1994

Leaving the Cotswolds, an area of outstanding natural beauty, for war-ravaged Yugoslavia was not as easy a decision as I had initially thought, but I felt it was the right opportunity. Early that Friday, Mum and Dad drove me to the Land Rover plant in Solihull, near

Coventry. Finding the armoured vehicle section was a challenge; the whole manufacturing plant was spread over a large area with some departments in new, state-of-the-art buildings and others tucked away in Second World War factory buildings complete with peeling camouflage paint and long-vacant bomb shelters. At one building, we spotted a small sign on a side door that read "Armoured Vehicle Department". Mum and Dad wished me luck and left me outside the door. It was starting to rain, so I walked in and there, lined up neatly against one side of the spotless, brilliantly lit workshop, were five brand-new, three-tonne, shiny white Land Rovers. The price tag of each vehicle was close to 50,000 British pounds. Just looking at them, I knew this was going to be a grand adventure. I didn't consider the war we were heading in to or the scenes of carnage and destruction shown on the television each night. No, not me. I was just thrilled to be on my way.

En route to Zagreb with armoured Land Rovers – Slovenia, 1994

The four other drivers soon turned up. One, an ex-army guy, gave each of us an envelope containing 300 British pounds for expenses on the trip to Zagreb. The envelope also contained a note from the BRC, directing us to keep all receipts because we would need to account for the money at the end of mission when we returned to the UK.

The trip through Europe took three uneventful days. Only when we crossed from Austria into Slovenia did we encounter unploughed, snow-covered roads, making driving a bit more challenging.

The Land Rover has always been one of, if not the best off-road vehicles. But the two tonnes of extra weight, because of the armoured panels, affected the handling and four-wheel drive capability. The vehicles felt top heavy and liable to tip over if used in the off-road mode. As I later discovered, when they did crash, the armoured panels simply fell off. Two weeks later, a high-velocity sniper's round tested the integrity of one of these armoured windscreens. The driver and passenger were unharmed because the full metal jacket projectile was absorbed by the seventy-millimetre-thick multi-layered glass. The ICRC generally used unarmoured Toyota Land Cruisers for day-to-day work. If an armoured four-wheel-drive vehicle was needed, Land Rovers were the answer because their heavier build made them more capable of carrying the extra weight. We later found out that these Land Rovers were destined for use in Sarajevo, the besieged capital of Bosnia and Herzegovina, where four-wheel drive manoeuvrability was not so important, but armour plating was.

Upon entering Slovenia, I was expecting to see some evidence of the war, but everything looked just the same as the last time I had passed through the country ten years earlier.

CHAPTER 2

Base Training Zagreb

* * * * *

Sunday, February 13, 1994, 10 p.m.

Eventually, we arrived in Zagreb; locating the ICRC offices was difficult in the dark, but we found our destination by hailing and following a local taxi. Every delegation had a Welcome Desk, which ensured arriving personnel had accommodation waiting for them. Even at this late hour, someone was on duty. After we handed over the documents and keys for the Land Rovers, we were taken to an ICRC guesthouse, the first of many I would come to use. The fridges were kept stocked with bread, milk and cheese, so whatever time one arrived, there would be something to eat and drink.

Back at the delegation early the next morning, the four of us, minus the fifth driver, who delivered his Land Rover and then flew straight back to the UK, met up with thirty other drivers who had

7

also recently arrived from all over the world. We visited all the relevant departments to pick up our equipment and our essential ICRC Blue Book Pass (ICRC pass). Signing for the allocated equipment we were told everything must be returned upon finishing our mission, or the cost of missing items would be deducted from our pay.

Issued was a camping stove, fuel and stove repair kit, camping utensils (knife, fork, spoon, cup and kettle), a sleeping bag and a comprehensive medical kit. By then, I was beginning to wonder, *What kind of adventure will this be, given the amount of stuff they've handed out?*

We also received a new, white Kevlar helmet and a Kevlar flak jacket; only good for protecting the torso from small pieces of spent shrapnel. (The heavier bulletproof jackets were issued depending on the situation you were going into.) And yes: two Russian-manufactured field shell dressings that "must always" be carried in the two front pockets of the flak jacket; this also gave me pause for thought. With all of us carrying this stuff around, the light-hearted banter became a little strained and muted as we realized this trip to war might actually become dangerous.

For the next four days, between regular visits to the local bar, christened the "sub-delegation", we went through an intense training program consisting of truck and trailer driving in the local hills, snow chain use, wheel changes and how to couple and uncouple trailers and semi-trailers. I knew all this truck-driving stuff but thought it prudent to keep quiet, *I might learn something.* A couple of drivers sent over by their National Societies had truck-driving experience only operating snowploughs on airport runways. To the BRC's credit, they always sent experienced blokes.

The most interesting part of this training was the additional three days we spent at the Mobile Army Surgical Hospital (MASH) being trained by an American Vietnam vet doctor in the art of field medicine. The Basic Military Field Medic Course was usually held over a ten-day period, but due to the demands of the war, for us, it was packed into three days.

The course started out as good fun and a huge laugh until the doctor, chisel-jawed and granite-eyed, shouted in his best parade ground voice, "Gentlemen, sit down, shut the fuck up and listen to me!" Then, in a more conciliatory tone, he said, "I have three days to train you guys, and at the end of the three days, you will leave here trained and able to stop someone from dying." He added smiling, "Well, at least until someone with more brains turns up and saves the day."

This had the desired effect. We sat down, faced forward and shut up. We spent the next three twelve-hour days watching graphic Vietnam War footage, then discussing what we would do, who we would try to save, and who would be left to expire on the battlefield. Most of us got it wrong: the guy you thought you could save should have been left to die, and the guy you thought was doomed to die was the one to save. At the end of the third day, just as we were thinking the diploma would look damn good on the mantle, the instructor, whom we all called "The Dear Doctor", handed out to each of us white-faced drivers a full intravenous injection kit.

"No bastard leaves here until I see a functioning drip in each left arm. So, pair up and inject one another!"

Well, this got me thinking, *Should I try and do it myself or get my neighbour to? Best get the Irish guy opposite me to do it. Then at least I can look away during the process.* His hands were not just shaking; they were positively fluttering like he was doing a bird impression. Eventually, he jammed the needle into what we both agreed looked very much like a vein. The saline solution was turned on and started flowing into my battered arm. Feeling somewhat refreshed, I started to stab around in his arm and, by some miracle, soon found a vein, turned on the little plastic tap and, *voila*, my very pale partner began the first steps on the long road to recovery – at least until we got to the bar.

The ICRC Zagreb training program also covered how to deal with the many types of militias; including military, paramilitary, police, bandits and anyone else, drunk or sober, who wanted to interfere with our assignment in delivering relief goods. I found this part of the training very interesting. Most of the scenarios discussed were exactly what I had encountered on my previous travels in the Middle East. The difference this time was that now we were forbidden to offer any sort of bribe to get things done.

* * *

A few months later, while stationed in the Serbian capital of Belgrade, I met an ICRC delegate who had worked in Africa over many years. He told me that on one mission in Liberia, he had to negotiate a checkpoint manned by drug-addled child soldiers. The information he passed on to me over the next month was to prove invaluable after I ceased truck driving and became a convoyer. He said that you must try to change the balance of power during your negotiations with dangerous, frightened, unpredictable, weapon-carrying soldiers, or worse, armed children.

He recalled that he would almost daily have to run the gauntlet of threats, violence, intimidation and theft until he discovered that the child soldiers manning the checkpoint only wanted to go back to school and study. The next day, armed with notebooks, he explained to them he could help them with their studies. To each gun-toting youth, he gave a list of simple arithmetic questions, a pencil and an eraser. "I will mark your work tomorrow," he promised. The following day, he had four of these former unprincipled killers meekly lining up to have their work marked and receive the exercise for the next day. He had no more problems at that checkpoint.

He had changed the balance of power.

When escorting a convoy, I would often be flagged down and told to move to the side of the road by two or three soldier-bandits waving assault rifles and demanding a payment of sorts to allow us to proceed, maybe twenty German Deutsche Marks (DM) or a packet of smokes. We called these incidents "flying checkpoints". I knew, as did the opportunist checkpoint operators, that what they were doing was totally illegal – just robbery at gunpoint. One time I was flagged down, I tried an experiment.

Sure enough, en route to Tuzla with a ten-truck convoy, I was flagged down and motioned to pull over. Radioing the convoy, I instructed them not to pull over but to stop in the middle of the road right behind me. With the road nicely blocked, I slowly climbed out of the Cruiser and asked what the problem was.

"You must pay a toll to use this road," bellowed one shifty-eyed fat guy wearing gumboots and waving his rusty shotgun around in a most unsoldierly manner.

"What you are doing is illegal," I replied, "and I will report you to the nearest military authorities."

As the seconds turned to minutes and other traffic began to back up, he became increasingly agitated. Then two Bosnian Croat forces (HVO) soldiers got out of their Jeep and started to walk to the front to see what the holdup was. Seeing this, the toll collector almost begged me to leave and clear the road. In the minute it took me to get in, start the engine and let my guys know we were leaving, the would-be extortionist had vanished into the woods. Back on the road, my field officer and I had a good chuckle.

I had changed the balance of power, and it felt good.

★   ★   ★

By February 19th, we were trained and ready for work. The thirty-four of us were on standby, to go out on convoy at anytime, anywhere in the former Yugoslavia. Four days later, my excitement was beginning to fade; this was becoming a hurry-up-and-wait scenario. But on the morning of the fifth day, nine others and I were notified and briefed for a ten-truck convoy to Zenica, in Central Bosnia; we would leave at five the following morning. Before the war, a summer trip from Zagreb to Zenica took seven hours. During winter, it took a few hours longer but was still possible within a day. With the main

ROGER JOHN FOWLER

UNPROFOR Lifeline Routes – 1994 (Map courtesy of nationsonline.org)

12

roads and bridges either under direct artillery observation, closed with barriers, mined or destroyed, the trip now took two days.

The United Nations Protection Forces (UNPROFOR) had developed a system of routes across the country, using dirt back roads and forest trails. UNPROFOR road repair crews with bulldozers, graders and ploughs, often working shifts around the clock, kept these roads open. The twenty-seven routes were named, and conditions for their access could change daily.

A daily notification read:

- Diamond – closed after 6 p.m. High risk of banditry.
- Pacman – UN Canbat. Need 24-hour notice.
- Square – open. Often closed due to mines at Doljani.
- Skoda – closed. Bridge collapsed and a mine barrier closed the Busovača T-junction.
- Mario – closed. Bridge collapsed.
- Gannet – open. UN checkpoints established south of Mostar.
- Hawk – open. Route in very poor state of repair. Rigid body vehicles only.
- Acorn – mostly open. Light vehicles only due to mudslide and damaged bridge.
- Monk – closed due to landslide.

At the appointed time, we were lined up at the ICRC warehouse, sitting in our trucks waiting for the convoyer to position himself at the head of the column and give us the signal to start. Never having driven in a convoy before, I wondered how the day would go.

We knew the convoy rules, and I hoped all of us would remember them:

- Keep the truck behind you and in front of you in sight.
- Keep a safe distance from the truck in front.
- Do not stop unless instructed by convoyer.

- Most importantly, listen to the VHF radio for any instructions.

We were scheduled to spend the first night in Banja Luka in Northern Bosnia, which according to a pre-war census, was home to a multi-ethnic mix of 623,000 Serbs, 356,000 Muslims and 179,000 Croatians. During the war, approximately ninety percent of the Muslim population and eighty-five percent of the Croatian population fled, fearing for their lives at the hands of the de facto Bosnian Serb authorities. To erase any traces of the former residents that they were expelling or killing, these authorities blew up and destroyed all sixteen of the city's mosques, one a masterpiece of sixteenth-century Ottoman architecture.

Seven hours later, after spending over an hour waiting for our convoyer to negotiate safe passage with the Bosnian Serb Army (BSA) into the town of Banja Luka, we headed to the ICRC warehouse and parked the trucks inside. We managed to find space for all of us in the rear of the convoyer's Land Cruiser and were taken to one of the few remaining, relatively undamaged houses that the ICRC rented as drivers' overnight accommodation. I noticed that one wall opposite the bedroom window showed some blast and shrapnel damage. Just one month previously, a hand grenade had been thrown through the window; luckily, no one was there at the time. The window and blind had been replaced, and I really hoped it wouldn't happen again, especially when we were sleeping there. I returned to Banja Luka many times, but the feeling I had then of darkness, fear and pervasive evil did not diminish; I was never comfortable in that town. I was relieved the following morning when we drove out in convoy towards Zenica where we would deliver our load of food parcels and medical goods.

Zenica is a large industrial hub well known for its vast steel works; it had suffered from some of the worst atrocities during the early part of the war, from 1992 to 1994. For eighteen months, this fourth largest city in Bosnia and Herzegovina with a population of 96,000, the majority of which were Muslim, had no water or electricity. It was widely reported that many of its citizens died from sniper fire and hunger. At noon on April 12, 1993, the HVO fired six 155-millimetre-artillery rounds into the central bazaar, killing fifteen and injuring fifty people. Almost every night, the BSA positioned in the surrounding hills would fire at random, one or two high-explosive rounds into the town.

Eleven-truck convoy into Bosnia, 1994 (J. Forbes)

Lying in my cold bed at the end of day, listening to the explosions, I wondered what carnage was being brought down on the citizens and internally displaced persons (IDPs) who sought safety in the city. Oddly, I never felt in any real danger from this random shelling. I found the atmosphere in Zenica much less threatening and oppressive than that of Banja Luka; although we were advised to avoid certain parts of the city due to the presence of the Mujahidin, whom the Muslims were not happy to have in their country. I observed that cities like Banja Luka, controlled by Bosnian Serb authorities, posed the highest threat to the civilian inhabitants.

Unloading the trucks in the warehouse that evening took several hours, and we were all glad, after twelve hours on the road, to get to our accommodation. By five the next morning, we were ready to start on the return trip. With empty trucks and no hold ups, we got back to Zagreb later that day.

From a Sitrep the following day:

> *Two American F-16 jets shot down four Serbian G-4 Super Galeb Light-Attack Aircraft, which were violating the UN no-fly zone over Banja Luka and attempting to make their escape after bombing the military factory at Novi Travnik.*

This two-seater trainer and light-attack aircraft, powered by the superb Rolls Royce Viper turbo jet engine, could be fitted with a centre line twenty-three-millimetre twin-barrel cannon with the ability to carry up to 590 kilograms of wing-mounted ordnance. These planes were no match for the vastly more powerful American F-16 jets.

The tense atmosphere in Banja Luka was much worse after this event.

★　★　★

Three weeks later, a United Nations High Commission for Refugees (UNHCR) Danish relief convoy of ten trucks left Banja Luka heading to Tuzla in northeast Bosnia. Sixteen kilometres into the journey at a BSA checkpoint near the HVO front line, the UN convoyer was told to return and bring back the correct documents; and to leave the convoy with the soldiers at the checkpoint. The convoyer and his translator returned a few hours later in a local police vehicle, having had his own UN Land Cruiser and radios confiscated by the police. A Danish UN driver, who attempted to call for help on his VHF radio, was dragged out of his cab and onto the road. The BSA colonel in charge ordered all the drivers out of their trucks and took their keys. He then ordered the drivers to walk back the sixteen kilometres to Banja Luka. And they began their trek, in single file, guarded by armed soldiers.

The situation was extremely tense; after the drivers had walked three kilometres towards Banja Luka, a BSA truck stopped and marshalled all ten drivers into the back of the truck. They were then taken to a house a little farther on. Later, they were told they must walk back to the still-guarded convoy. When they arrived, the drivers saw that all their personal belongings had been removed from their trucks. Just then, another BSA truck arrived, and the drivers, who were by now very worried about what might happen to them, were ordered to get in the back and to, "Keep your heads down because of snipers."

Near the front line, at another abandoned house, they were lined up against a wall, instructed to empty their pockets. When the drivers saw the soldiers gather their belongings and throw them in a heap, they were petrified and presumed they would be killed, as had happened to others. They were then marched twenty minutes to the front line and directed down a path that crossed a minefield, being told to keep low, talk loudly and wave their white shirts. After one kilometre, they arrived, to the amazement of the Croatian soldiers on duty, at an HVO observation post on the other side of "no man's land". The UN soon sent vehicles to collect their terrified drivers and take them to the UNPROFOR base at Žepče, Central Bosnia.

This was an extreme case of intimidation. Most convoys travelling in the former Yugoslavia during this war had similar, although somewhat less frightening, tales to tell.

★ ★ ★

Over the next two months, we ran twenty-four four-to-twelve-truck convoys into all areas across the former Yugoslavia. The convoys contained seed potatoes for distribution to local farmers so they would have a crop for the next year; we also carried medical supplies, individual food parcels, blankets, tents, water bladders, hygiene kits and water-sanitation equipment.

At the time, the relief operation was the largest and most complicated undertaken by the UN and the ICRC. The United Nations High Commissioner for Refugees (UNHCR) was operating for the first time in their history in the middle of an open conflict, as were other humanitarian organizations. For the ICRC, this was familiar ground.

With some three million people displaced, 500,000 had fled to neighbouring countries, leaving over two and a half million people in need of help. By the end of the conflict, the UNHCR had delivered over 950,000 tonnes of supplies, with 160 tonnes of food airlifted to Sarajevo. Also, by war's end – protracted or not, wars do eventually end – the ICRC had delivered over 100,000 tonnes of relief supplies and spent over forty-eight million Swiss francs (CHF) on medical assistance. In 1993, this Swiss organization spent fifty percent of its entire global budget in the former Yugoslavia. What they were able to achieve with a budget of 378 million CHF was truly phenomenal.

I drove in many convoys containing medical supplies from Zagreb to Bihać. On one trip to the Bihać Hospital, during the unloading of ten tonnes of medical supplies, the Army of Republika Srpska

(ARSK) started with the daily shelling of the town. I had left my flak jacket and helmet behind in Zagreb, which was to become a worrisome trend. A shell landed one kilometre away, with the next seven rounds advancing towards us by 100 metres each time. I watched the reaction of the hospital staff, rushing to get me unloaded and on my way. They became more worried after each detonation. Just as we decided to take cover, the shelling stopped as suddenly as it had started.

Ten minutes later, two young boys offered me a large piece of still-warm razor-sharp shrapnel; I gave them each a pack of Marlboro cigarettes in exchange. They would sell the cigarettes. I kept the shrapnel as a souvenir, and it is still sharp enough to shave with.

The random shelling was nerve-wracking for its civilian targets, as it was intended to be. Everyone exposed to this type of assault suffered in one way or another; the people of Bihać went through it almost daily for years. It is also a war crime.

From a daily Sitrep:

> *The north of the area of responsibility was calmer with 114 detonations heard to the northeast of Velika Kladuša. Troop movement continued between Velika Kladuša and Mala Kladuša. The south, continuing to be active with thirteen shells impacting in and around the Bihać area. Two tank shells impacted in Bihać town. Detonations were heard in the area of Grabež, Klokot and Vedro Polje; a repeat attack was launched by five corps BiH on Velika Skokaj. The situation is still very tense with both warring factions reinforcing their positions.*

I found it difficult to imagine how ordinary people continued with their daily lives with this stuff happening every day for several years. As I tried to understand the people and their culture, it seemed to me that this arranged marriage of the former Yugoslavia was always on the brink of a very nasty divorce.

★ ★ ★

In the Bihać area, there was an intriguing military air base built inside Plješivica Mountain. The base was started in 1948 and completed in 1967. Over six and a half billion US dollars (USD) was spent building one of the most sophisticated air bases in Europe. It could survive a direct hit from a twenty-kiloton nuclear bomb and had four 100-tonne pressurized doors guarding over three and a half kilometres of underground runways. It was completely self-contained, with its own water supply, accommodation, food and supplies for 1,000 personnel. This marvel was financed and built by the former Yugoslavian military.

Operating from this base, which contained a full workshop and repair facilities, were two squadrons of the latest Soviet MiG-21 fighters. The base was used extensively by the Yugoslav National Army (JNA) from 1990 through 1992 to conduct operations at the start of the Yugoslav Wars. The JNA partially destroyed the base when they withdrew to consolidate their forces in Serbia. One year later, ARSK forces completed the destruction with a staggering fifty-six tonnes of explosives, shaking the nearby city of Bihać.

★ ★ ★

CHAPTER 3
A Lovely, Pale-Blue Lady's Bike

● ● ● ● ●

After twenty-four convoys, each one different, I was getting into my stride and thoroughly enjoying every minute of the work. I still thought it was a jolly good adventure. Not surprisingly, the terrible hardships and suffering we witnessed and were, to a degree, involved with began to affect most, if not all of us, in different ways. Many of the drivers were drinking every night. It was becoming clear to me that this sort of humanitarian relief work, with the long hours and constant strain in a war zone, encouraged some to drink more than was healthy. Drinking with the guys was obligatory, but the thought of tomorrow morning's four-thirty alarm had me tucked up in bed before midnight.

One evening, on a convoy to Split, my very drunk English friend was getting worked up over his girlfriend's flirting and he started a fight with the bloke who was paying attention to her. I frogmarched him out of the bar and onto a small dock, telling him not to drink so much, and "By the way, don't fall off the dock." Just as I said this, he fell in with a loud splash, went to bed soaked through and woke up feeling much the worse for wear.

Post-traumatic stress disorder was not talked much about at the time, but it most certainly was displayed by many personnel. My mind was already full of images of war, and I was determined not to use alcohol to cope. I decided on a plan.

Each Sunday, there was a large flea market in Zagreb. There, I bought a second-hand, pale-blue lady's bicycle for the princely sum of forty-five DM. When I was not out on convoy, instead of spending my time with the others in the sub-delegation, I would get out my bike and explore the city; cycling around Zagreb was relaxing in the spring weather.

Pale-blue lady's bike – Split, 1994

★ ★ ★

Cycling was my thing. As a young lad, I cycled more of the Wiltshire countryside than many people had driven. I entered road races organized locally by the Swindon Road Club and had a favourite coach who instilled in me a passion for the beauty of cycling. As a sport, cycling was affordable, and I received my first new bike on my thirteenth birthday. It was a ten-speed beauty, with dropped handlebars and I rode it every spare moment I had. My nan had a holiday chalet on the south coast of England; each summer my mum, dad and we four kids would make the six-hour trip in Dad's car. That summer, I announced to everyone that I'd cycle to West Bay. One hundred and sixty-one kilometres and fourteen hours later, I arrived: exhausted yet elated that patience and determination could take me anywhere. I was to repeat a similar proclamation nearly thirty years later as I planned for my return from my mission in the former Yugoslavia. Cycling saved me, physically and mentally, during my mission.

★ ★ ★

When I was based in Split, I spent my spare time either swimming, exploring or cycling out of town on my lovely, pale-blue lady's bike, supplied with a bottle of water, a hunk of bread and a piece of cheese. I'd spend all day in the sun, with the warm wind blowing in from the sea, just wandering across the Dinaric Alps, high above the Dalmatian coast. I would hide my bike behind a bush and was always pleasantly surprised when I returned from my hike and found it where I left it.

One day I discovered a deserted monastery, half built into the mountainside. It was completely empty except for one room where I found a magnificent white marble table, beautifully and intricately carved. This table must have been in the same room for centuries. I believed it was still there because of its great weight – I guessed 400 to 500 kilograms of solid marble. I often wondered how the original monks managed to get it up the side of the mountain and into the building; seeing no roads or tracks anywhere nearby. I wonder if it is still there.

On another hike, on the same mountain range, I came across a large piece of naval shrapnel, most probably fired from a warship during the Second World War. Thoroughly rusted after lying undisturbed on the mountain for fifty-five years, it would have been a lovely souvenir, but was just too heavy to carry. I had to leave it where it most likely remains.

My #2 stress-relieving tactic was walking. When on convoy, at the end of the day, instead of heading to the nearest smoke-filled and soldier-packed bar, I would, if it were reasonably safe, go for a walk. During my time on mission, I walked many kilometres and explored many villages, towns and cities. The "reasonably safe rule" was sometimes stretched a little, but walking was a terrific stress-reducer.

Mostar, 1994

One wet Saturday afternoon, I found myself waiting on the Muslim side of Mostar, in southern Bosnia and Herzegovina, to collect an ICRC delegate at his end of mission and take him to Split to continue his journey home. Wandering through the almost-deserted, destroyed and bomb-blasted town, I headed along the old Turkish bazaar street – littered with thousands of pieces of rusting shrapnel, roof tiles and shattered glass – towards the Stari Most. This historic work of art was, in 1557, the widest man-made single-arch bridge in the world. The bridge was the symbol of Mostar, spanning the Neretva River and connecting the Croatian and Muslim sections of the city. It had been aggressively targeted for destruction by the HVO, another sad case of cultural property destruction.

Pre-war Stari Most – Mostar (postcard c. 1990)

The Stari Most was commissioned by Suleiman the Magnificent and designed by a Turkish architect involved in designing many of the sultan's buildings in Istanbul. It is said that on completion and before the scaffolding was removed, the architect made preparations for his funeral, should the bridge collapse.

War will destroy just about anything, but for me, the destruction of this beautiful bridge was a testament to what little was held sacred in this conflict. After standing for nearly 500 years, on November 9, 1993, at a quarter past ten in the morning, having received sixty direct hits, Stari Most fell into the green and roaring Neretva River.

The UN Spanbat had erected a wire pedestrian suspension bridge as a temporary measure. This had also been hit by artillery fire, blowing off half the wooden planks laid on the deck but leaving the two upper and two lower steel cables intact – without a walkway – stretched nice and tight over the river.

I decided that I would walk over the bridge just until the walkway ended, then turn around and walk back. But at the end of the walkway, I wondered if I could get right across to the Croatian side. The bomb damage didn't seem to have affected the suspension cables, so with my feet on the wet lower cable, my grip on the equally wet upper cable became more of a death grip the farther out I went. Halfway over, I happened to look down; the sight of the rushing torrent of water crashing over the jumble of rocks thirty metres below made me realize this was not one of my best decisions. This was a stupid place for Roger to die.

About then it dawned on me that not many months previously this was one of the most dangerous spots in the whole of the country for sniper activity from both sides of the town. If I had been in the cross hairs of someone's telescopic-sighted sniper rifle, they must have decided to let this clearly unbalanced Englishman live another day. Safely on the other side, I decided to rethink my reasonably safe rule.

CHAPTER 4
Falling For Split

* * * * *

April 23, 1994

Good news: I was being sent to the port city of Split, where I would be based. It seemed that Split was expanding its relief operations and Zagreb was scaling down. I didn't know for sure, but it may have had something to do with Split being a little closer to Central Bosnia. Each time I had been to Split on convoy, I liked the place more and more. A fourth-century Roman palace and fortress situated in the town centre was surrounded by charming Italian-style buildings with cosy restaurants and cafés tucked away in the polished-marble-paved medieval streets. And the best bit was our accommodation: a pension three kilometres out of town on the road to Makarska, one of many old Adriatic ports, and right on the beach.

The pension, Mikuličić, was owned and operated by a young couple who always made us feel welcome. After spending three or four sixteen-hour days on convoy, getting back to my Adriatic water-front room and being lulled to sleep by the sound of the waves was sheer bliss. Much nicer than nights spent in Central Bosnia lying in a cold bed listening to and wondering where the next, random artillery round might land.

The Adriatic – wearing obligatory swimming safety helmet! 1994

June 2nd

We had a new Croatian currency, the Kuna. It was much needed because the old Republika Hrvatska (Croatian) dinar was suffering from enormous inflation, as high as 1,500 percent. The most common currencies in use were the DM, British pound, CHF, or USD instead of the local currency, but the DM was king.

As well, inflation skyrocketed for the Bosnian dinar. Overnight a ten dinar note became 100,000 dinars; the bank simply stamped the new amount over top of the original note. One day a bottle of beer cost forty dinars; the next day it cost 400,000. People on a fixed income, including pensioners, if lucky enough to receive their monthly pension, became destitute. After this drastic devaluation, the average monthly pension was barely enough to buy a bar of soap if one could be found to buy.

Devalued Bosnian dinar

We watched the terrible events unfolding in Rwanda between the Tutsi and the core Hutu political elite on television in the Split delegation. The ICRC were organizing a large part of the truck fleet, including expat drivers, to deploy to Rwanda from Split. The workload from Split remained high, but because the political situation between Croatia and Bosnia and Herzegovina was more settled, the need for all expat drivers was not so urgent and local Croatian drivers were being employed to go on convoy into Bosnia.

All expat drivers were on standby to go to Rwanda, and although I was somewhat excited, I was also a little anxious having seen the gruesome news footage of the genocide. I was hoping the ICRC had forgotten about me and would leave me in Split. Each day we heard of more drivers being shipped out to Rwanda, and I knew my turn would come sooner or later.

One sunny day, we were informed that all the Split expat drivers were to drive to the north of the country, cross into Italy at the Trieste border, then drive the three-day trip to the Italian port of Brindisi on the heel of Italy, for passage to Rwanda. I was just starting to figure out how I could avoid going there, leaving this paradise behind, when the Irish Relief Delegate patted me on the shoulder and said with a grin, "But not you, Roger." I wondered if a public hug would be acceptable. Probably not, so struggling to keep my happiness from showing, I simply nodded and said nonchalantly, "Oh, why is that?"

Three weeks previously ICRC Zagreb decided there was a need for an expat driver to work in Serbia, therefore I handed over my passport for a Serbian Visa application. My passport was apparently still sitting in the Belgrade Embassy passport office; without a passport, I was unable to go to Italy. I was relieved to miss the trip to Africa. What the guys witnessed and went through there defies description. The few I met in Zagreb during their return debriefing were not the same people as when they left three months previously to go to Rwanda.

After the drivers' departure, the Split drivers were now Croatian – except our convoyer, Bob Milne, an Englishman whom I knew from my trips to Iraq and Saudi Arabia back in the seventies; Johnny Forbes, a Canadian from Nova Scotia; and me. The three of us were attempting to learn Serbo-Croat. This was now the language spoken on convoy, not English. To hear the drivers cursing in their language was rather entertaining; most of the time I got the gist of conversations but occasionally I needed a more detailed explanation.

Our days started at 5 a.m. and were spent on the road taking relief supplies into Mostar, Jablanica, Zenica and Tuzla with the occasional trip into South Krajina, where we had a small sub-delegation in the town of Knin. As expat drivers, we took supplies into Knin because our Croatian drivers couldn't cross into the Serb-held enclave.

Route Diamond – Bosnia, 1994 (J. Forbes)

On the mountain routes during the hot, dry summer months, we choked on the thick clouds of dust despite moving at a walking pace trying to negotiate the narrow, loose-surfaced track euphemistically called a route. The truck directly in front often disappeared from sight, and there were times our wheels were centimetres away from the edge of a nearly vertical drop of hundreds of metres into the valleys below. The wrecked trucks that had failed to stay on the track and took the quick way down, paid mute tribute to the price paid by the unfortunate drivers.

There were many times I held the door open ready to jump if the wheels failed to grip and the truck started to go over. We heaved a collective sigh of relief when eventually the road levelled out, just before we attempted the next treacherous mountain pass. Always alert for rock falls and washouts, we coaxed our trucks along past particularly difficult sections; small wonder we were exhausted at the end of each day. This work tested everyone's skill, stamina and nerve. As frightening as driving in the summer was, the winter convoys were much more challenging; dealing with the snow and ice on the mountainous sections was often truly terrifying.

When I did get back to Split early enough, a swim in the sparkling Adriatic made everything right again, and I was ready for the following early start back into Central Bosnia. The ICRC Split warehouse staff worked equally long and arduous days loading and preparing the trucks, often till late into the night. Juric, our warehouse manager, would always be there at the start to make sure we had everything we needed for the trip. He was our quiet-spoken hero.

On the return trip from a long, but ultimately unsuccessful ten-truck convoy to the enclave of Gorazde where we were denied entry, at the last checkpoint I received a radio call asking me to go to Zagreb first thing in the morning to collect my passport, complete with Serbian Visa, and go to work in Belgrade.

I knew it was likely that I would eventually go to Belgrade, but again, I was hoping ICRC Zagreb had somehow forgotten about me. Still Belgrade would be a lot nicer than Rwanda. I did wonder how the guys were doing there. That evening I packed my two small bags. With all the travelling around since my arrival, staying at many different guesthouses, I had become an expert on travelling light. The next morning at the Split delegation I said my goodbyes. Feeling a little sad about leaving, I was driven to the airport, where I caught a Croatian Airlines Boeing 737 for the one-hour flight north.

CHAPTER 5
Belgrade

⬤ ⬤ ⬤ ⬤ ⬤

At the ICRC Zagreb Welcome Desk, I collected my newly stamped passport, a bag containing 15,000 DM in used notes and three large bags of "tracing mail", all for delivery to the ICRC Belgrade Administrator. The tracing mail was more important than the large amount of cash because it was the lifeline for families separated by the war and desperate to reunite, or at the very least, to have closure regarding the whereabouts of their loved ones. There was a clean, shiny Land Cruiser waiting for me; feeling quite important, I drove off on the 400-kilometre trip to Belgrade.

The E75 Motorway, locally known as the *Autoput*, between Zagreb and Belgrade had been closed to civilian traffic since the beginning of the war. Only the UN and other humanitarian organizations were able to use this route, except during active fighting. The only other route was a two-day journey north into Hungary, then east and then down into Serbia. There had been no recent reports of warring activity, so I decided to use the *Autoput*. There were two semi-permanent checkpoints built across what was a busy four-lane road linking Europe to Turkey and the Middle East. I had travelled this route many times in the seventies and eighties. Now I saw that service stations were destroyed, crash barriers flattened, and the occasional shell crater in the tarmac, and weeds taking over where cars, buses and trucks once roared past, going about their business. The desolate scene as I drove along on the beautiful mid-July morning would have made the perfect backdrop for a film about Armageddon.

Two hours later, I could see the first checkpoint. This marked the end of Croatian territory and the start of the buffer zone between the warring parties: every war has its "no man's land" – land that is under dispute, left unoccupied as a buffer zone. The term is commonly associated with the First World War to describe the area between two enemy trench systems. No man's land in the Yugoslav Wars typically held two checkpoints at each crossing, one Serbian and one Bosnian and/or Croatian. Sometimes there was a third checkpoint between the belligerents, manned by the UN.

At the barrier, I stopped and kept my engine running just in case I needed to move quickly. I waited for a soldier to come out of the ramshackle, green-tarp-covered shack. Five minutes passed, and I saw no one. Sitting for three or four days at a time on checkpoint duty, in the middle of nowhere, these guys often started drinking early in the evening and thus got up late. I often thought if I were the enemy, I would launch a midnight raid any day of the week, and sneak in and capture the post. Snag was, the soldiers on the other side had also started drinking every evening and were in no condition to do any such thing. It was apparently more fun to lob a few mortar rounds over during the day after both sides had a chance to have a bit of breakfast, a smoke and sober up.

A murderous-looking guy eventually came out of the shack, stared at my ICRC pass and, with a plum-brandy-laden belch enlivened with just a whiff of garlic, said, *"Dobro utro kako ste?"* (Good morning, how are you?)

"Dobro, dobro hvala." (Good, good, thank you.)

Then, with a cheerful, *"Sretan put"* (Safe journey), he lifted the faded black-and-yellow barrier and waved me through. This just went to prove that looks, coupled with nervous tension, whether you admitted it or not, could be deceiving.

The one-kilometre drive across no man's land was rather eerie. The road was in horrid condition, with much mortar-round damage and some larger artillery craters. The craters were full of weeds, showing that the damage was not recent. The road was strewn with rusting pieces of shrapnel; and some of the larger trees on the side of the road had been blasted limbless. It was quiet and still. Trying to avoid the larger pieces of shrapnel, I had no choice but to drive over the smaller pieces and hope I didn't get a puncture. As instructed, I would never leave the road, no matter how strewn with rubbish, for fear of hitting any planted land mines.

At the next checkpoint, Serbian Ockuchani, the blood-shot-eyed soldiers were already out of bed, unshaven, smoking and standing out in the sunshine, manning the post like all good soldiers did. I got out and checked my tires for damage; they seemed to be fine. The soldiers glanced at my pass and waved me through, on my way to Belgrade. For the next 250 kilometres, I saw only the occasional Serbian Army vehicle, and civilian tractor crossing the deserted motorway to get to the next field. Five hours later, I was at the outskirts of Belgrade, which had a completely different feel and atmosphere to Zagreb. It felt dark and sombre. The large Soviet-era-built city centre was vastly different than the modern glass-fronted Zagreb.

★ ★ ★

Years before, on my trips to the Middle East, I had always looked forward to getting into Serbia. There were several large, state-owned transport companies on the approaches to Belgrade, one of which was called Yugo Sped. Foreign trucks were welcome to call in and visit the 24-hour canteen and enjoy simple, wholesome food at no cost. I was always hungry, and after a pleasant and filling meal, I could go for the next day or two on my usual truck-driving diet of chocolate, Coca-Cola and cigarettes. A lot has been said comparing the communist system to the West, but this free cafeteria food and acceptance of a foreigner calling in and eating as much as he could, seemed a great idea. It certainly had a positive impact on me and my stomach.

★　★　★

The ICRC Belgrade delegation was almost as difficult to find as the Zagreb offices, but after driving around the city for what seemed an eternity, I found them tucked away near the massive thirty-square-kilometre cemetery. Parking outside, I grabbed the bag of cash and the three bags of tracing mail and went straight to the administrator to hand them over. After a quick introduction to the few staff not out in the field, one of them drove me to my new accommodation. I would be sharing the apartment with a Canadian driver, Paul, who had been in Belgrade for a couple of months. Later, he explained there was not a lot happening, and life was tedious.

And tedious it was. Each morning, there was a briefing at the delegation that all expatriate staff had to attend and make their report. Although mandatory and not particularly informative, the briefings were the venue for an impressive performance. Midway through, the Swiss Head of Delegation would pause and slowly scan the room, not looking at anyone specifically, but making sure we were all awake and paying attention. Then, with the timing of an Oscar-nominated film star, he would reach into the top, left-hand pocket of his immaculately pressed shirt and slowly remove a stylishly crumpled, but almost full pack of extra-strength Camel cigarettes; with a well-practised, almost imperceptible flick of the wrist, he'd produce a smoke. Simultaneously, his well-worn but still shiny Zippo lighter would somehow appear. With another flick of his wrist, the dangling cigarette would be lit. At his desk, reclining back in his chair, he would then exhale and look through the blue smoke at each of us in turn. "What do you think of that then?" his eyes would ask. I almost applauded but stopped when I noticed the others' stifled yawns. I never tired of watching the daily performance over and over and over.

The tracing team always had something to report: how many Red Cross Messages had been delivered, the number of families that had been traced and reunited, as well as updates on prison visits. The medical and logistics reports, however, were inevitably, "Nothing to report, we are still waiting to get access to Srebrenica, Zepa and Gorazde." Our focus was to try and get access into these three enclaves, but this was proving next to impossible due to the military and political situation.

From a Sitrep:

> In April 1993, after eleven months of indiscriminate shelling and many civilian deaths, the UN declared Gorazde a "safe area" designed to protect the civilian population. This had no deterrent at all on the besieging forces that continued to wage war on the local population, killing five hundred and eleven civilians.
>
> One year after the UN declared Gorazde a safe area, the BSA were in a position to overrun the town having captured the Gradina Heights and advancing to within one and a half kilometres of the town centre. After holding out for two long years against overwhelming firepower, the lightly manned Muslim defenders were being pushed back, unable to withstand the violence of this latest attack. With rumours of beheadings and reports from fleeing civilians of whole

villages being systematically destroyed, the population was close to being in a total panic. After hearing of UN personnel being targeted, as well as the very real risk of the town being overrun, Lieutenant-General Sir Michael Rose, commanding the UN peacekeepers, requested a targeted NATO airstrike against three BSA artillery positions targeting the town. Within twenty minutes, the shelling ceased, forcing the BSA to pull their forces back twenty kilometres from the town.

I was involved in one failed attempt to bring aid into this beleaguered town. The BSA then determined to repeat the same assault on Srebrenica with gruesome results.

ICRC Belgrade had been trying to gain access to Srebrenica for many months before I arrived and were still trying. Every few days, we would leave with two or three trucks loaded with humanitarian aid, having all the notifications and paperwork necessary for access to the town. After spending four hours at the checkpoint, we were predictably turned back.

On August 4, 1994, our field nurse – an English doctor on loan from the BRC – and I had at last managed to get through the BSA checkpoint and into Srebrenica. Our two Land Cruisers were packed full of sorely needed goods for the Bosnian Red Cross medical personnel still able to function amid the isolation and starvation.

Driving past the Dutchbat Base in the Potcari Battery Factory five kilometres outside the town, we soon came to Srebrenica. There were hundreds and hundreds of refugees and displaced persons, simply standing, sitting and lying around, some under tarps, others with a makeshift structure to shelter under from the relentless sun. Many had nothing. All the haunted people I saw on the drive through the town were ragged and thin. For many, this was the end of the road. They had seen their relatives and friends slaughtered and their villages burnt to the ground. This town, designated a safe area by the all-powerful UN, was their last hope. I could not believe this was happening in Europe. The scene before me was the same as the newsreels about the Second World War, but in colour.

The two local Red Cross staff, struggling to keep the tiny clinic open, were shocked and surprised to see us at their door. With tears of gratitude and sadness, they explained they had almost lost hope and were nearing the end of their strength to continue with the clinic. "Something bad will happen soon, and everyone fears for their lives," they said. We soon had our medical goods unloaded, and Amira offered us Turkish coffee laid out on a broken, dark wood coffee table, covered with a worn plastic cloth. Before the war, there would have been several plates of biscuits and sweet sticky Turkish treats. Today, there were four small cakes on offer. Adin apologized. "Please take one," he insisted. We both did out of courtesy and respect for the local custom. Sipping our coffee, I knew this was the only hot drink they would have that day due to the shortages. The clinic was simply the front room of one of the few undamaged houses. The water supply was intermittent, depending on the mood of the surrounding BSA and it could be cut off for hours, days or weeks. We were told there had not been any water for five weeks, and no electricity for at least twelve months. The clinic was situated on the main street; to one side, there was a small stream running down from high in the hills. This water was the only supply for the 70,000 inhabitants trying to stay alive.

I was intrigued to see set in the stream dozens of bicycle wheels fixed on makeshift stands, and small plastic paddles screwed on the tireless rims being turned by the power of the water. A small wire ran into the houses providing at least some electricity for a dim light. I felt relieved to leave for the two-hour trip back to Belgrade. There was such a terrible feeling of impending doom in the whole town.

The next few weeks, we experienced the same nonsense with the authorities as we continued to try to get access to the enclaves of Srebrenica, Zepa and Gorazde.

The dance on a typical weekly attempt went something like this:

- With all the necessary documentation in order and all military authorities notified, we left early, hoping to catch the checkpoint guards before they started their daily drinking.
- Two hours later, once again, I sat waiting with two other trucks parked just before the Serbian checkpoint, watching our intrepid convoyer duck under the camouflage tarp, knowing he would be in with the soldiers for some time, attempting to gain access.
- An hour later, he reappeared and, trying to control his anger, informed us that we needed to turn our convoy around and return to Belgrade.
- "The paperwork is once again not in order," he said through clenched teeth out of earshot of the soldiers. "I've been drinking plum brandy with them for at least an hour, hoping to win them over to let us pass. This bullshit must be coming from a much higher authority than these guys."
- After some difficulty turning the trucks around, we headed back to the Belgrade warehouse, where we unloaded the trucks, again.

At first, I didn't understand why the military authorities gave us permission and then refused us entry. I surmised that they wanted to be seen to be doing the right thing.

Meanwhile, thousands were starving and dying in the town, which was, of course, the authorities' plan all along. I knew this aid was sorely needed and felt powerless at not being able to do anything except meekly turn around and go back.

★ ★ ★

Ten months later, the unimaginable did happen: the worst mass murder on European soil since the Second World War. General Ratko Mladic, known as the "Butcher of Bosnia", was the enthusiast at the helm for what would be known as the Srebrenica Genocide. In 2017, he received a sentence of life imprisonment for committing war crimes, crimes against humanity and genocide from the International Criminal Tribunal for the former Yugoslavia.

This small mountain town of 22,000 residents had grown, with the addition of 48,000 refugees and IDPs, to over 70,000 people. For more than three years, the population had been cut off from the rest of Bosnia and the rest of the world, bombed, starved and murdered. These were some of the poor souls the ICRC was trying to help.

On April 16, 1993, Srebrenica became the first declared UN Safe Area in the conflict. A safe area is meant to protect its inhabitants from any armed conflict or any hostile act. A small UNPROFOR Dutchbat contingent of 370 men was based in the town but did little to protect the local population during the twelve-day genocide two years and three months later. I believed, along with others, that the Serb authorities wanted to rid Srebrenica and its environs, amounting at one time to 900 square kilometres, of all the Muslim inhabitants. The common phrase for this is ethnic cleansing.

From July 11 to 22, 1995, 8,372 men and boys were murdered. They were hunted down in the wooded hills while trying to cover the seventy kilometres to get to safety across the border into Tuzla. Many of the murdered were locked in farm and industrial buildings, then shot and burnt alive. All this is well-documented; few managed to escape and tell the world what was happening.

I was based in Split at the time of the genocide. On July 22ⁿᵈ we received an urgent call from the Tuzla delegation. The request was that our Split field nurse be flown there immediately in a UN helicopter to collect an inexperienced ICRC Swiss delegate. Over the previous twelve days, this young woman had been trying to document the stories being told to her by survivors, many of the tens of thousands of women and children fleeing the genocide. As she listened to the atrocities committed just over the border by the Serbs, she simply lost her mind. Our field nurse (from the Icelandic Red Cross) flew to Tuzla, put her colleague in a straitjacket and within a few hours flew her directly to Switzerland, where she was hospitalized. I could not imagine any one of us not having a similar reaction to hearing those horrific accounts. Our delegate was brave to have listened so intently to these outpourings of grief and fear.

When on mission and thinking about the fighting in this war, and specifically the genocide of Srebrenica, an eerie scene presented to me:

> The dark wind of war had gathered momentum and turned into a maelstrom of hate on its fitful journey towards the town. If I listened carefully, I could hear mothers wailing. Breathing deeply, I knew I would smell the soon-to-be spilt blood. This wind had occupied the troubled skies of Yugoslavia during the protracted war, looking for another village, town or hamlet to appear on the dark horizon, to continue with the grisly task of murder and butchery. Sighted for destruction were Srebrenica, its 296 surrounding villages and their inhabitants.

It was hard to believe these atrocities were happening so close to Belgrade during a seemingly normal July. Almost a year later, I recalled the observation of our ICRC Knin Swiss delegate, also quite young; her impression was that Europeans did not truly comprehend the magnitude of this war. She hypothesized that such atrocities might occur in other places in the world, but how could this possibly happen in Europe? It was simply too close to home; if occurring here, similar atrocities could occur in other parts of the continent as well. She thought that Europe chose to ignore this war because it was the business of the former Yugoslavia, and the fighting and politics were too complicated. If it was ignored, it might just go away.

I had applied for membership to the American Embassy Club in Belgrade and was surprised when I'd been accepted. To get into this elite club was not easy, but I think being an ICRC delegate most certainly helped. I made sure I wrote "ICRC delegate", and not "ICRC truck driver" on the application form. I had been in this club a couple of times during my previous journeys to the Middle East. As far as I could tell, nothing had changed in those years, except there were now ninety security personnel for thirty diplomatic staff.

It was always a pleasant experience to go and sit at the bar, or at a white linen-covered table and just relax in the sophisticated atmosphere. As a member, I could sign in a friend, so one night my roommate Paul and I decided to go and have a few beers and a burger. The beer and burger were great, especially in the air-conditioned restaurant, but I could not help feeling guilty when I remembered the starving and frightened people just a short, two-hour drive away in Srebrenica.

★   ★   ★

I think all wars must contain the same movements, with people carrying on as best they can with their everyday lives. After lives are lost and property is destroyed, the survivors pick up the pieces, move on and try to resume living as before.

On one of my many trips into Sector North, while passing through scenes of pure destruction, I saw village after burnt-out village. There was not a soul to be seen – no animals, no people, nothing. I was wondering when all this devastation had occurred and where all the inhabitants were, when I saw coming toward me a driving school car with a young woman in the driver's seat. She was, while gripping with white knuckles and her chin on the wheel, taking what I presumed to be her first driving lesson. I thought it was a mirage. However, it was evident that life does indeed go on, and this young lady just wanted to learn how to drive.

On another occasion, not expecting a normal-life experience upon entering the town of Tuzla one afternoon, I was leading what had been a long and arduous winter convoy from Zenica. The Serbian artillery started to fire on the town, following their usual pattern of random firing; first one, and then three or four, stop for ten minutes, then fire ten shells one after another. Then, as was often the case, simply stop the bombardment. There was never any rhyme or reason to this sort of thing except to keep everyone on edge. The sensible thing to do when artillery was being fired was to take cover. As we were only two minutes from the warehouse, I decided the safest thing would be to continue and wait out the attack at the warehouse. In the centre of town, the police waved me down, and I radioed to the drivers to also pull over and await instructions. I didn't factor in the police stopping me and giving me a two DM fine to be paid right there and then, in cash, for not wearing a seat belt. Shelling or not, civilian rules were to be followed, and the fine was rather reasonable.

★   ★   ★

People trapped in places like Zenica and Tuzla were enduring terrible hardships from lack of medical care, water, food and, in the winter, fuel for cooking and heating. In severe contrast, one day, Paul and I each took an empty truck up to Zagreb via Hungary. The Autoput motorway was completely closed due to renewed fighting, thus our route through Hungary. It was a pleasant, two-day trip involving one night in a truck stop on the way, then down into Zagreb the following day. It was great to drive through Hungary and see a country at peace and not destroyed by war.

★   ★   ★

When I first went to Belgrade, another Brit working for the ICRC asked me to visit a relative of his wife and see if I could help her out with anything. "But be very discreet when you go. Either get a lift with someone or, if you take a Land Cruiser, park a few streets away and walk to the apartment, preferably after dark." The relative's name was Vesna.

She was the single mother of a one-year-old daughter. Before the war, she had an apartment and a job. Neither the job nor the apartment was very good, but still, she had a life and friends. Soon after the war started, she was evicted because she was Croatian. With nowhere to go and friendless, she asked her neighbours if they would allow her to camp out in the basement of her previous apartment, and they *graciously* agreed. So, this was the address given to me, along with the cautious instructions. I had no idea what to expect or take to her, but I thought a bit of food would be welcome.

That first night, carrying a bag with a loaf of bread, cheese and a few tomatoes, I parked a couple of blocks away and made my way into a run-down, Soviet-style, high-rise housing estate. The pavement bars were full. As I passed each one, the young unemployed men sitting on plastic lawn chairs under the harsh glare and hiss of kerosene pressure lamps gave me a look that asked, "Who are you, and what are you doing here?" This put me on edge, especially when I didn't really know where the apartment was. I certainly didn't want to ask anyone and draw any more attention to myself or the ICRC. Each concrete tenement block looked exactly like the next. There seemed to be no power available in this part of the city; the only light was from candles or, if one could afford the fuel, from pressure lamps. Although I could read the Cyrillic alphabet a little, mostly by recognizing the shape of the words (so maybe *read* is not the correct term), it was difficult in the gloom to make anything out. I was about to give up and head back to the Cruiser; if I could remember where I had parked it and if it had not already been stolen. Standing in the shadows, trying to decide what to do, an old lady came shuffling out of one of the tenements, so I asked her for directions to the particular block I was looking for. With a questioning look, she pointed across the road.

Trying to be as quiet as possible, I found the graffiti-covered steel door to the basement. Calling out and pushing it open, I looked in and saw a dim light shining from under a door to what looked like the janitor's storage room. I remember my friend telling me that Vesna lived in such a room. She opened her door and asked who was there. My Serbo-Croat language skills were not too good, but after showing her my ICRC pass and mentioning my friend and his wife, she realized who I was and invited me into where she had been living for the past ten months.

She and her daughter lived in the storage room where they shared a mattress. She had a two-ring burner for cooking, no bathroom and just the janitor's sink for washing. The temperature and humidity in the squalid basement were hard for me to take, having just come in from outside, and I wondered how they could stand the heat.

I spent an hour trying to converse with her; I could see that the child was not well. The next visit, I brought some food for the child, fruit, and vitamins. Vesna told me that she was suffering from some type of cancer and could not get treatment because she was Croatian.

I made many visits to the janitor's room during my stay in Belgrade, taking food, medicines, a little cash and some clothing for them. Each time, I snuck in and out under cover of the hot and oppressive Serbian summer nights. If it became known that she was receiving foodstuffs and gifts, she would be a target for theft and perhaps much worse. The night before I left Belgrade for the last time, I asked Paul if he would continue in my place helping Vesna with whatever he could. I never spoke with him after that, as one month later he ended his mission and returned home to the east coast of Canada. I hoped he was able to visit her.

I was bored almost to death in Belgrade and was seriously considering applying to work as a convoy driver for the UN. I had a couple of acquaintances working for them, and they said they were busy and that the pay was good. However, working for the ICRC was quite prestigious and, as we were not the usual run-of-the-mill relief agency, we received a lot of respect because of our professionalism, stellar history and dedication. The Red Cross logo looked good too. The locals were wary of the UN and equated it to a government military organization. In contrast, the ICRC could get into places and sit at negotiating tables that the UN and other agencies could not. I learned that the International Red Cross Movement was the author of the Geneva Conventions and that these treaties and protocols established the standards of international humanitarian law in times of armed conflict.

★   ★   ★

Another thing I learned on mission was how to cook – well, almost. Because of the sanctions imposed by the West on the Serbian government to stop supporting the breakaway Republika Srpska, the Serbian economy was suffering, especially with food and fuel supplies. Basic food like vegetables, mostly potatoes, was still available, but the quality and variety were poor. To help the expat and local staff, ICRC Belgrade gave each of us, each week, a box of American Army, sometimes British Army, ration packs. The full ration packs were worth having because they contained goodies like cigarettes, chewing gum, chocolate, toilet paper and powdered soft drink sachets, along with the main meal – beef or chicken – in a thick, brown boil-in-the-bag skin. These meals were designed to last at least twenty years and were almost inedible. Each week we received a box of five of these meals, minus the goodies.

So, one Saturday afternoon, I boldly said to my roommate, "Paul, I'll cook us a proper dinner tonight. I'll do cauliflower cheese." At the local market, we spotted what looked like a nice, fresh, firm cauliflower. After another search, we found a lump of cheese; I didn't know what sort of cheese, but it looked fine. Back at the apartment, we were almost dizzy with excitement, knowing soon there would be a plate of hot cauliflower cheese on the table.

How hard could this stuff be to make anyway? With the oven turned on, we thought it would be best if the cauliflower was washed before cooking. We set it in an appropriately sized, slightly chipped but serviceable casserole dish, cut the cheese into thin slices and placed it gently on top. Then we carefully put our creation into the oven. We were both very pleased with our culinary skills and decided a beer would be in order. After we emptied each bottle, we checked the cauliflower. All seemed fine. The cheese was melting spectacularly and smelled heavenly. The first seeds of doubt came at bottle number three (or was it four?), when I decided to stick in a knife and check how tender our veg was. Must not over-cook it, of course. Luckily, my cooking partner had his back turned, busily opening another bottle for us to enjoy, when I realized something was very wrong. The knife would not penetrate. As we were still in a celebratory mood, I thought it best to keep quiet about this. By this time, the cheese was on the verge of igniting, so we removed the cauliflower from the oven, sat it on top of the stove and waited for it to cool before tucking in. During the cooling period, I hoped the softening process would occur. After half an hour, it seemed cool enough to dish up.

Sadly, this was not possible; the cauliflower had refused to cook. After a few more beers and some well-cooked cheese, we decided it must have been a faulty cauliflower.

★　★　★

CHAPTER 6
The Chicken Farm

* * * * *

August 22, 1994

A good day: Paul and I were leaving the boredom of Belgrade. There was a crisis happening in the hamlet of Batnoga, which had a pre-war population of 300. It was located in the short-lived and unrecognized autonomous state of Western Bosnia (1993–1995), the capital of which was a small town of 52,000, Velika Kladuša. Former Bosnian President Fikret Abdić was trying to carve out a kingdom for himself and rule Western Bosnia. He succeeded for two years by employing cult-like propaganda tactics, including lies, deception and intimidation.

Overnight, a large, abandoned chicken farm on the outskirts of Batnoga was filled with 20,000 displaced persons from Velika Kladuša and the surrounding villages after the ARSK launched a major attack in the area. I didn't know why they ended up at this abandoned farm, but I did know that they were in desperate need of help. There were another 20,000 displaced persons living in equally squalid conditions in a makeshift camp near the village of Turanj.

I was relieved to be leaving Belgrade and going back to Zagreb. The E75 Motorway was again open for the UN and other non-governmental organizations (NGOs). We headed out on what promised to be another hot, late-August day. We were held up for two hours at the Ockuchani checkpoint for no good reason, but there was absolutely no point in getting annoyed when these delays occurred. The soldiers would simply make you wait for another two hours. If you got them cross enough, they'd turn you around and send you back the way you came. I had learned frustrated patience during my travels while negotiating the many border controls on my previous trips to the Middle East. Eventually, the "gate keepers" tire of the game and let you pass. Finding the Zagreb delegation had not got any easier but, driving round the city in ever-decreasing circles, find it we did. The Welcome Desk gave us the address of what would be our accommodation for the time we'd be there.

It was past midnight when we got to our digs. There was a power cut, and the guesthouse was in total darkness. Neither of us had a flashlight, but having stayed there a few times before, I knew where the beds were, the bathroom and the well-stocked fridge. We were both hungry, and finding by touch, wolfed down some bread, cheese and bottled water. Up early the next morning, it looked like another beautiful day. When I went to the fridge for more bread and cheese for breakfast, I was shocked to see the cheese had mould spots, and the bread was completely covered in a carpet of green. I felt fine and Paul reported no ill effects.

Wisely skipping breakfast, we went out to the Land Cruiser parked right outside. The whole vehicle had been smeared with what looked like human excrement. Paul, on the verge of throwing up just looking at this stuff all over the windows, lights and most of the bodywork, could not go near the vehicle. *If I can open the door, we can drive to the ICRC workshop and power wash this poop off,* I thought. By now, we were late for work. To my despair, I saw that all the door handles had been covered as well. Paul, having regained his composure, was watching me as I crept closer to see if our original assumption was correct. Dear Paul almost passed out when I reached out and touched some of the goop, then tasted it. Close up, I could see it was just chocolate cake. Why someone would waste perfectly good cake was beyond me. At the workshop, the guys had a huge laugh and quickly washed the vehicle. Ten minutes later, we were in the delegation. The pranksters' identity remained a mystery.

The previous night, the Welcome Desk had advised us that we would be extremely busy for the next twenty-four hours. There were thousands of people in need of food, water, shelter and medical attention at the Batnoga Chicken Farm.

Paul's truck was already loaded with food, blankets and tarps. He would deliver this to sub-delegation Velika Kladuša. My work was to collect the water tanker from the warehouse and go directly to the chicken farm and fill our water bladders, which had been taken to the camp late the previous night by the local staff based in Vojnić. There were six 500-litre bladders spread around the farm but no way of filling them until I brought the water tanker from Zagreb. Because of the urgent need for our delegates to be at the camp, there was no one available to escort me through the Serb-Bosnian checkpoints. I had none of the usual notification and no documents. Regardless, at both checkpoints, the soldiers lifted the barriers and let me through. I thought both sides realized if they hindered the ICRC and UN, they would have to deal with this catastrophe themselves; not having the interest, will or capacity to do so, they let me pass.

Three hours later, I arrived at the Batnoga Camp. I faced an overwhelming number of people. Some of the lucky ones had set up in the empty chicken sheds after trying to clean the filth from the concrete, so they could at least have somewhere to lie down. Some were so exhausted they simply sat and stared, unable to hear the cries and anguish from the majority who, with their families, had only a piece of wet, muddy ground to lie on.

New York Times, November 13, 1994:

> *Wycliffe Songwa, a Kenyan UNHCR official involved with this madness says, "For me this is the shame of Europe. If I were back in Africa, I would understand, because the poverty is such that these situations arise. But in the middle of Europe, this is unacceptable.[3]"*

Eventually, I managed to make radio contact with the ICRC Water-Sanitation (Wat-San) Engineer and his field officer. He had been at the site for the last three days, trying to have open pit latrines dug by hand or machine, and was under extreme pressure. They had been working till midnight, then back at five the following morning. The UN had a backhoe on the site, but it was kept busy digging rubbish pits and keeping the muddy tracks open and passable. This was proving an almost impossible task due to the heavy rain, not helped by 20,000 pairs of feet churning the saturated soil into liquid mud.

He gave me directions to the water bladders and asked me to fill them as quickly as possible. After three days, the lack of water was becoming serious. After much slipping and sliding getting to the first bladder, I realized I didn't have a clue how to operate the pumps and hoses on the tanker. So, I connected an outlet hose and let gravity fill them. Much slower than using the pump, but at least some water was available. Halfway through the day, the sun came out and started to dry things a little, but the sour odour of unwashed bodies and excrement burgeoned.

---

3 https://www.nytimes.com/1994/11/13/world/for-rebel-bosnis-muslims-life-in-chicken-coops.html

Filling the six bladders took me until mid-afternoon; by that time, the others were half empty because of the demand. There was no way of replenishing the water in the tanker, as the local town's fire brigade depot, where we would usually fill up, had been destroyed in the recent fighting which was continuing not many kilometres away. I could hear the artillery explosions and heavy machine-gun fire sounding like it was just over the next hill.

I was surprised to see Paul arrive with his load of food, blankets and tarps. The fighting was too severe for him to deliver to the ICRC Velika Kladuša warehouse, so it was decided to bring his load directly to the camp. At the UN field hospital, on one of the few dry areas of the sprawling camp, with the help of four local young men, we started to unload the truck. By the time everything had been unloaded and stacked on pallets, it was dark, and we were exhausted. Just then, four other young men came running into the partially ready field hospital carrying a very old lady on a stretcher. There didn't seem to be much wrong with her, judging by the way she was bellowing and swearing as they went past me through the canvas door into the hospital. I could see they were laughing and good-naturedly shouting insults back at the patient.

After dark, people lit small fires for a little warmth and to cook on. Dotted across the fields glowed thousands of small, smoky fires, with families, including babies and elderly grandparents, huddled together on the still-wet ground. The murmur of 20,000 voices, and the smell and smoke clinging to the damp grass, produced scenes of biblical proportions. I saw one soldier with a stomach wound being comforted by his distraught girlfriend, kneeling in the mud beside him. I don't know if he survived or even if he managed to get to the newly erected field hospital. I hoped that he did. I will never forget that evening.

It was almost one in the morning, and we had been working for seventeen hours. Our delegate thanked us and suggested we return to Zagreb in Paul's truck, leaving the water tanker; a local Red Cross driver knew how to operate the pumping system and would continue as soon as they could get the tank refilled. The UN had things mostly under control, and with the situation stabilized, our part in the relief operation was finished. The ICRC would continue in the camp with the tracing team's work.

The drive back to Zagreb and through both checkpoints was easy. The same guys were on duty, but fast asleep. They were not very happy being woken at 3 a.m., but when they realized we were returning empty to Zagreb, they lifted the barriers and let us through, eager to get back to bed.

At five that morning, we left the truck at the warehouse and got a lift back to our accommodation. We had been working close to twenty-two hours and were beyond exhausted. Six hours later, a local Red Cross driver came around to wake us up and take us back to the warehouse, where we were each given an empty truck. Both were needed that day back down the E74 to Belgrade. My truck was an armoured Scania destined for Sarajevo. We arrived at the ICRC Belgrade warehouse much later that evening and after getting a lift to our accommodation, we slept on and off for the next twenty hours.

It was a luxury just lying around catching up on our sleep, making tea, reading or dozing. We eventually got a call from administration; we were expected to attend the briefing the following morning.

There, I was informed that the ICRC Split Relief Department needed a convoyer to replace the chap who had finished his six-month mission and was returning to Germany, and that I was his replacement. I knew him from Zagreb, where he had a good reputation and I hoped I would be able to fill his shoes and not let the BRC down. I was honoured to be offered the job. Driving trucks in convoy, summer and winter, was in itself a challenge, not for the faint of heart or the inexperienced. From what I had seen of the convoyer's job, it would involve more demands, including closer contact with all sides of the conflict. Always ready for a challenge, I was keen to get started and get back to Split. I had now been on mission for seven months.

CHAPTER 7

A Little White Coffin

✤ ✤ ✤ ✤ ✤

The day after being informed that I would be returning to Split, I was once again heading up to Zagreb from Belgrade, loaded with Red Cross mail and diplomatic bags. I quickly passed both Serbian and Croatian checkpoints. The soldiers manning them remembered me and didn't give me any trouble. It was pouring with rain when I arrived, and there was a distinct autumnal feel in the air, which was much better than the humidity in Belgrade. I was feeling great, knowing I would be in sunny Split within a few days. But first, there was work to be done from Zagreb.

The delegation was a hive of activity, dealing with the ongoing situation in the Batnoga and Turanj camps, in addition to resumed fighting in the area. The tracing team conducted the bulk of the ICRC work in the camps; they also read the messages to ensure they did not contain any military information and then tracing the mail recipients commenced. Then, we hoped, successful family contact would be the result. The tracing team was only twelve strong, so the volume of work generated by the 40,000 IDPs in the camps was almost overwhelming.

September 5th

I had a day off, and my plan was to do nothing but sit around, drink tea and doze. This humanitarian business was rather tiring, so no activity that day for Roger. Besides, there was still heavy fighting around Velika Kladuša, and I was scheduled to go there the next day on the mail run.

In the delegation, there was a small secure room under the stairs, where all the tracing and diplomatic mail was stored until distributed to the sub-delegations across the country. As well, anything of a sensitive nature was stored in this room. For the past few days, I had noticed a small white coffin placed off to the side in one corner. I was informed that the coffin held a child, who had died in the Zagreb hospital and was to be returned to the grieving Muslim family in Bihać. Each time I walked past, I glanced in, hoping to find that the little coffin had been delivered. But it was still there the morning I was to go on the mail run.

That morning, the UN Sitrep from ICRC Velika Kladuša stated that the fighting had ceased and was not expected to resume for a couple of days; it should be safe to deliver the mail. With my Land Cruiser loaded, I was eager to get away and see if the fighting had actually stopped, or if it was just a pause in the proceedings to enable both sides to replenish their food and ammunition. I should receive a call on the VHF radio if hostilities resumed, but the message often didn't get to me in time, so it was best to keep my eyes and ears open for any change, however subtle. For example, was the local bar open or closed? Were there more or fewer people out and about, or was it quieter than usual? It was a good idea to have both windows rolled down enough to hear what might be shouted at you as you drove by, or to be able to hear if fighting had resumed ahead or on either side of you. Also, it was good not to have music blaring from the radio, unless it was Bob Dylan, of course! Just as I was ready to leave, to my dismay, I was handed the little white coffin with instructions to deliver it to the Bihać Hospital morgue.

At noon, I arrived at ICRC Velika Kladuša. As I handed over the mailbags, the staff informed me the front had moved towards Bihać and away from town. I was advised to take care on the trip to ICRC Vojnić; there were reports of sniper activity on the road.

The trip to Vojnić took ninety minutes. The countryside was strangely quiet and deserted. Passing several well-camouflaged T-55 main battle tanks and 135-millimetre artillery pieces, I could see the soldiers were alert and ready for action. To my relief, the snipers were busy elsewhere. Red Cross vehicles had been targeted in this war, but for the most part, all belligerents respected the Red Cross emblem and neutrality. The staff at ICRC Vojnić were happy to see me again but were clearly worried about the coming few days and weeks. It seemed that the tempo of the war in this sector was ratcheting up bit by bit.

The staff made me a cup of herbal tea and a salami sandwich and told me to take care on my way to my last stop, the Bihać Pocket. I don't like salami sandwiches but would never say so. The tea and sandwiches were more than food and drink; they said, "*We like you, Roger. Take care.*" The fighting had been heavy all week and although quiet at the moment, it could erupt at any time. I said goodbye, and off I went, with the little white coffin secured on the floor of the Land Cruiser by the Bihać mailbags and all the other equipment. The route I took would avoid the main checkpoints but was only suitable for four-wheel-drive vehicles.

ICRC Vojnić team, 1994

With Bob Dylan's "Blowin' in the Wind" cranked up to full volume, I edged down off the road onto a section of the dried-out River Una. This route was not the official way into the Bihać Pocket, but so long as we, the Red Cross, took just one vehicle and not too often, the soldiers manning the guns on both sides turned a blind eye. I was never totally comfortable taking this route; any day, the rules could change, and we might end up being fired upon. I carefully followed the tire tracks under the gaze of the ARSK gunners besieging the town and avoided the washed-out and soft mud areas. Without warning, the gunners started firing their OGANJ 128-millimetre multiple rockets over my head. As usual, I had forgotten to bring along my flak jacket and helmet. Feeling a little exposed, I sped up, and the little coffin bounced around in the rear with the mail.

After panicking for a few moments, then realizing that the rockets were not aimed at me but into the town, I slowed down and took a breath, wondering, *What am I doing here?* With the rockets screaming overhead, sounding like an express train, and my sad little cargo, I continued across the riverbed towards Bihać, hoping the bombardment would stop before I got there.

I found the track up onto the opposite bank. At the first sturdy-looking tree, I stopped, got out and with my back to the rocket fire and the beautiful sound of Bob Dylan competing with the roar of the rockets, I made myself sit down to smoke a cigar. I absorbed the noise, the warmth of the sun, the smell of the grass and wondered what destruction the rockets were causing in the town I was about to enter. After a while, the bombardment stopped just as suddenly as it had started.

Driving through the town, I noticed a four-storey apartment block ablaze after being hit during the bombardment. I arrived at the hospital at the same time as some of the wounded. Eventually, I found the exhausted mortuary attendant amidst the chaos and said goodbye to the little white coffin. The attendant gently took it from me and carried it inside to await collection by the parents for a proper Muslim burial.

A few streets away at the delegation, I handed over the last of my mail bags, along with a few supplies for the staff. Common items in normal circumstances were impossible to obtain in Bihać during the war – a couple of cartons of Marlboro cigarettes, tea, coffee, a bunch of bananas, and bread fresh that morning from Zagreb. The staff needed a break from the siege that had been going on since June 1992; twenty-seven months later, there was no sign of it easing.

Taking the main road out of town, I noticed a few more buildings burning fiercely. The few remaining firemen drew on what little energy they had left, fighting the fires and at the same time listening for more rockets and shells to come their way. With an empty Cruiser, my trip back into Croatia took no time at all.

* * *

On one six-truck convoy into the Bihać Pocket with my load of medical supplies, my task was to go directly to the hospital while the others unloaded at the warehouse. When we had finished, one of the overworked doctors offered to show me around the hospital. Walking through the wards and corridors jam-packed with wounded soldiers and civilians alike, I knew then how essential our supplies were to the hospital and its patients. After this close-up tour, I understood a little more of how the staff were coping and realized the enormity of what was happening to Bihać and its population.

*   *   *

One cold and wet Sunday afternoon, a few months after dropping off my precious cargo, I found myself driving through Sector North on my way to Velika Kladuša. Out in the deserted countryside, I noticed a young mother standing in the rain, having been just dropped off by a local bus. A toddler stood by her side; in her arms, she held a baby, and at her feet were three large bags, all getting wetter by the minute. She was, I thought, a displaced person looking for shelter and safety. I cannot remember what I was doing or where I was heading, only that I was again in a hurry responding to an emergency call. What I wanted to do was stop and give her a lift to wherever she was going, but I didn't. I thought, *What is the Red Cross doing here if I don't have the time to help this woman?*

*   *   *

CHAPTER 8

Bosnia and Herzegovina

* * * * *

September 7, 1994

On my return from Bihać, I received a radio message from ICRC Zagreb saying I was to leave at three the next morning and go to Split to start my new job as convoyer. The fastest way from Zagreb to Split was southwest through Velika Kladuša in Sector North, then south towards Knin in Sector South, and finally west towards Split on the Dalmatian coast. The trip took approximately seven hours. Another route took seventeen hours and involved island hopping on four or five local ferries. I had travelled that route once but decided never to take it again because of how long it took.

Because of the fighting in Sector North, the only other route was west through the badly damaged town of Karlovac, then keeping in Croatian territory, southwest towards the coast. Just before Zadar, the Maslenica Bridge spanning the Karinsko River provided the only remaining direct road link between Zagreb and Split. However, on November 21, 1991, explosives destroyed it. I decided that I would take my chances crossing the UN-operated pontoon bridge that ran beside the shattered remains of the original bridge.

From ICRC Zagreb – important notice for drivers:

> *Following recent mishaps, everybody driving from Zagreb to Split and vice-versa is herewith reminded that the use of the Maslenica Bridge remains <u>strictly forbidden for all ICRC personnel,</u> considering the fact that the bridge and the roads approaching it are shelled virtually every day.*

The time saved by using the pontoon bridge was considerable. Taking this route many times with no mishaps, I was never questioned why my trips between Split and Zagreb were almost twice as fast as other drivers'. Leaving Zagreb as planned, I got to the Maslenica pontoon bridge around eight; I hoped it was too early for an ARSK gunner seven kilometres away to wake up, have a smoke and start his daily task of firing a forty-five kilogram, 155-millimetre, 1,000 USD, high-explosive shell over the Dinaric Mountain range onto the floating bridge. The bridge had been hit on several occasions, sinking some of the barges. It was about 310 metres long and had to be crossed very slowly. Anything faster than a walking pace, the barges began to sway and move about quite alarmingly, threatening to flip you off and into the ominous-looking water. Crossing was risky, and I was always prepared for an unexpected swim. But each time, I made it across safely.

Through the ancient port town of Zadar, then a scenic three-hour drive with the rocky coast on my left and the sparkling blue sea on my right. After eight months of working in difficult conditions, I was happy to be heading back to Split.

Compared with what the guys were going through in Rwanda, I had won the lottery.

At noon, I arrived in beautiful Split. At the delegation, I was intro-duced to the different departments: tracing, relief, radio room, administration and finally, the Head of Sub-Delegation, Maria. During my mission, I had been to Split many times and knew most of the ICRC local staff, including the workshop and warehouse crew. Wanting to avoid any mistakes, I thought now would be a good idea to understand how the delegation worked. All I really wanted to do was to go and say hello to the charming couple running the Pension Mikuličić and have a swim from their beach. Instead, I spent the rest of the day talking with everyone and learning the systems.

At the workshop, I met the manager, Juric, who was to become a good friend and ally. He took me to collect the Land Cruiser that would be mine as long as I was there; then I drove to my apartment just outside Split in the small seaside community of Stobreč.

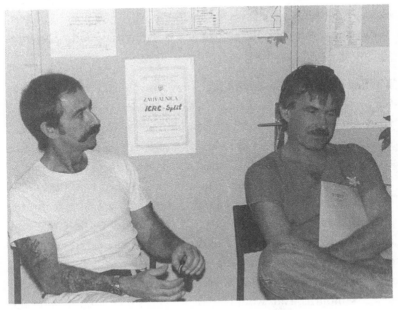

ICRC Split sub-delegation briefing, 1994 with Juric

There was a party that night at the Mikuličić for some expat staff based in Central Bosnia, who were on their way home after finishing their six-month mission. Three delegates had worked in Zenica and two in Tuzla. Both delegations were in Muslim territory and, because of the workload and stress, were classified as hardship postings. Chatting to the delegates, I deduced from the looks on their faces that one six-month mission was all anyone could take before a long break was needed.

The next few days passed in a blur of swimming, reading, dozing and eating in the many good restaurants on the Split waterfront. Over the following months, I attended many UN security briefings at their compound not too far from our warehouse. Each morning, from eight till nine, the briefing was conducted by a UN officer who shared reports of any warring activity, route closures and changes, and other incidents that had occurred over the previous twenty-four hours. All NGOs were expected to attend whenever possible. Later, at the delegation, I would inform Maria of anything of importance, including convoy security.

My first time as a convoyer, I had arranged to pick up the drivers at 5 a.m. and leave for the Zenica/Tuzla trip at six. There were just five trucks in the convoy, so the trip should be easy to manage. Later, I would run fourteen-truck convoys with ease, but for the first run, five trucks were quite enough – especially as my Serbo-Croat language skills were still a little weak. Ivan, my field officer, was a godsend, experienced and spoke perfect English. During the first few months, I relied heavily on his knowledge. Slowly, as my Serbo-Croat and route knowledge improved, I could actually make decisions on my own without constantly having to consult him. As the expat ICRC representative, my position as convoyer was senior to his. In those first few months, Ivan would gently suggest something, then let me pretend it was my idea, thereby maintaining the all-important chain of command.

For this first convoy, *we* decided to take Route Triangle into Central Bosnia, south down the coast road, crossing into Bosnia at Imotski, and then travel through Mostar, Jablanica, Prozor, Gornji Vakuf-Uskoplje, Bugojno, Travnik and Zenica. Then, from Zenica, we took Route Skoda through to Kakanj, Vareš, Kladanj, Ribnica, Banovici and finally Tuzla. I knew these places from the previous months of driving on many of the UN-maintained routes but had no idea how much more I would come to learn about them in the coming months.

A five-truck convoy into Bosnia from Split, 1995

After unloading four trucks in Zenica, we left the drivers to await our return. Escorting the fifth truck, Ivan and I drove on to Tuzla, unloaded and spent the night before returning to Zenica and continuing the trip back to Split. A large part of the route between Zenica and Tuzla was over dirt roads and logging tracks that had been churned into a fine, choking dust by the dozens of relief convoys. Fortunately, it had been raining, so the dust that could be worse than thick fog was not a problem. A little rain helped keep the dust down, but any more than a little and the tracks would turn into a quagmire. There were two options, dust or mud. This time we had mud.

Three days and 1,120 kilometres later, we were back in Split. This was not the norm for a convoy, as there was usually some accident, security incident, hold up, or breakdown. I felt really pleased the trip had gone so well.

Occupied bunker on Route Triangle – Bosnia, 1994

As convoyer, it was important to be one or two kilometres ahead of the convoy; if I came across any incidents, I could warn the drivers to pull up and wait until the situation had stabilized. Incidents didn't always stabilize, and sometimes worsened with the fighting intensifying. In these circumstances, I would radio the closest ICRC delegation, get available information and, if possible, be rerouted. If I could not raise anyone on the radio, it was my responsibility to decide what to do. Most of the time, patience and waiting paid off; the fighting would die down or move onto another area, allowing us to proceed.

On one return trip, with the convoy two kilometres behind me, I received an urgent radio message from ICRC Zenica telling me not to enter the town of Prozor because of heavy fighting. Unfortunately, we had just entered the town. I directed the convoy to pull over and wait. My field officer at the time was a young guy, Marko, who would fall asleep the second we left Split and remain sleeping for what seemed like the next three or four days until we returned. I slowed and stopped right in the middle of the town and woke Marko up to let him know what was going on. There was nobody around; the few bars were shuttered, the plastic chairs empty and waiting for the soldiers to return and continue drinking. I wound my window down, turned down the VHF and HF radios and just listened. I could hear some small-arms gunfire rattling around in the hills, but nothing going on in the town. After a few moments, I decided to call the drivers to come through as fast as was safe and go past me. Then, after the last truck passed, I would follow; when we were clear of the town, I would overtake and continue leading the convoy. This was a classic case of waiting, listening and then making a firm decision.

After each convoy, one of my duties was to write a full report for Maria and recommend any operational changes. During our debriefing following this convoy, she let me know that my decision to continue through Prozor was, in the circumstances, the correct one.

From a Sitrep:

> *Mostar: HVO capture JNA barracks during operation "Jackal". 90,000 Mostar residents flee for their lives.*

When I had time, and all my work was finished on my trips to Zenica, I would go for a walk into the city centre to stretch my legs and relax with a can of fizzy beer while sitting on a plastic lawn chair at one of the many pavement bars dotted along the main street. Summer was the nicest time to be there when all the young people would get dressed up and parade up and down, laughing, joking and showing off. Promenading had been a tradition even before the war; now, because there was no other entertainment available, the locals made an even bigger effort to look good and have fun, trying to forget their predicament. Often a group of young people would gather round someone with a guitar and sing beautiful, haunting melodies. Hearing these songs, I again felt privileged to be there.

One summer evening, sitting with a couple of my drivers at one of the bars, just watching the procession of young people, I heard singing. Across part of the street, a column of about thirty skinny young men and teenagers marched past, wearing an assortment of clothing. Some had on camouflage trousers; one wore what looked like his granddad's Second World War jacket and forage cap. Some wore old nylon rain jackets; some even had Yugoslav National Army (JNA) backpacks. All wore a motley selection of footwear – runners, dress shoes, army boots or rubber boots. And all were singing the American Army marching song "I Wanna be a Drill Instructor" as loudly as they could. While watching these mere boys, I felt so sorry for the suffering Muslims, who, with pitiful weapons, had to send boys off into the hills and valleys to be used as cannon fodder, many to die.

★   ★   ★

Wherever I travelled in the war-ravaged country, there was never a shortage of drink or cigarettes. To make money, one simply had to load a truck with American smokes, Ballantine or Johnny Walker whisky, not forgetting to have an extra supply for bribes, then drive into Bosnia, avoid the bombs, rockets, mines, gunfire and snipers, and sell it all for DMs, and then buy a farm. Enterprising, extreme-sport, death-wish risk-takers were doing this all the time. Some even survived to buy the farm.

Most ordinary people did not do this. Out of necessity, many would stand on the side of the road all day in the frost, snow, wind and rain wearing all the clothing they owned and try to sell a few packs of local smokes for next to nothing. The ones who made big money, maybe three or four DM a day, had a way of getting a few packs of Camel or Marlboro and then marking up the price one hundred percent.

I had the honour to get to know a young Muslim boy, Adin. When sitting in a sidewalk bar in Zenica one evening, I noticed a boy moving down the street calling into each bar, then a few minutes later emerging to go into the next bar. He journeyed down one side of the street, crossed the road and came up the other side exactly the same. A beautifully made and sturdy cardboard tray hung around his neck showing his wares for sale – perhaps two or three packs of local smokes, a few boxes of matches and maybe some chewing gum. That was Adin: ten years old and a real businessman. After an hour, he would be completely sold out. He'd disappear, then return ten minutes later with more stock in his cardboard tray.

Over many months I came to know Adin and would be disappointed when he didn't show up on his rounds. But most times, he was there, dodging in and out of the packed, smoky bars. I would often buy a pack of smokes and a pack of gum and pay with DM. The gum I would chew on convoy – better than chewing my nails; the smokes I would give away the next day.

One summer evening as Adin walked by and nodded to me, I saw he had a pack of real Marlboro in his tray; calling him over, I asked how much for the Marlboro. He looked me straight in the eye and said, "Three deutschemark." He then told me that sometimes they were available but not all the time, and he paid one and a half DM per pack. "A nice profit when they were available", he added.

At the French UN Battalion PX in Split, I could buy a carton of Marlboro for ten DM, so I figured I could help Adin expand his business. I would sell them to him for one and a half DM per pack and still cover my costs. This was a business deal after all, and Adin, who was doing all the footwork, made a clear profit of fifteen DM. After mulling over the offer, with a poker face, he said, "See me next week, and we can talk some more."

Knowing what Adin's decision would be, the following trip to Zenica, I had a carton of Marlboro tucked inside my jacket, ready to do the deal. Fifteen DM and the carton were exchanged with the dexterity of a professional Soviet spy, and Adin vanished. Ten minutes, later he was back. With a nod to his new business partner, he promptly sold the four packs of genuine Marlboro he had on his tray at the first bar. I had to admire this ten-year-old who was selling his wares and giving all his profit to his widowed mother. Some evenings he would have to go home and see her during his sales rounds; rather than carry his stock, he would trust me with his whole business. He'd leave it at my table with a nod, and off he would run. I would have defended that little cardboard tray with my life. I would love to know when he made his first million. Probably before he turned twenty.

*   *   *

One thrilling incident as convoyer: after unloading in Tuzla, I was asked to include in the convoy back to Split an old four-by-two Mercedes semi pulling an empty twelve-meter trailer. This truck had made the journey from Split to Tuzla two years previously before the main roads became too dangerous and were closed because of the fighting.

"Of course," said I, when really I should have said, "No way, we are just able to get through with the six-by-four Scanias!"

The driver was a local ICRC Tuzla employee who had family living in Split, and he was looking forward to seeing them. At almost every hairpin or steep turn, this totally unsuitable truck would get stuck. Running an empty truck was always difficult on loose surfaces because there was no weight over the drive wheels to provide traction. On one section of the track, there was a hairpin bend on a hill, too tight for the driver to be able to take a run at. He would get halfway round, and his wheels would just spin to a stop. It was risky having a complete convoy stopped, possibly a target for some long-range artillery practice. I figured the only way was to put snow chains on the truck and on all four of my Land Cruiser wheels. I directed Marko to reverse back down the hill and connect a good stout chain to the front of the truck, put the Cruiser in low range four-by-four, and then put tension on the chain. At my signal, both he and the worried-looking driver were to gun their motors.

"Don't stop till you get round and up over the hill," I urged.

Off they went, dust and stones flying. At the apex of the turn, the trailer became jammed against the rock face, but both vehicles had enough momentum to catapult the rear of the trailer out and over a fifty-metre drop, clearing the hairpin bend. Standing on a rocky outcrop at the top of the hill, I had a beautiful view of all this.

"Keep going!" I urged Marko over my hand-held VHF radio.

I had never seen a Land Cruiser do what this one was doing. The vehicle was actually hopping up the hill, pulling the ridiculous twelve-tonne Mercedes truck. As the wheels found some traction, they both would surge forward, then the chain would slacken off as the Cruiser wheels lost grip. Then they would jump at least ten centimetres, grip again and surge forward. Finally, we got to the top of the hill. After four hours, we were clear of the mountains and made good time to Zenica and on to Split, where we thankfully parked the old truck in a corner of the ICRC warehouse.

These situations brought out the best in me. Truly this incident was bloody good fun, manoeuvring the trailer around corners and up the mountain!

★ ★ ★

At the approach to most towns and villages we travelled through, there was often a line of mothers with their children, hands outstretched, hoping for something to be thrown from a convoy truck.

The UN and Red Cross drivers were expressly prohibited from this practice of tossing out treats; many children, trying to retrieve a packet of gum before the following truck barrelled down, sadly were run over. To some degree, this continued throughout the war. The kids and adults would point to their open mouths and yell "bonbons!" or pretend to be smoking, pointing to the invisible cigarette.

Driving through a particular village, I noticed that the footwear of the inhabitants was terrible. I asked my sister to send a variety of used shoes and boots from car-boot sales in England, and she did not disappoint. So, when it was safe, our drivers would slow down and safely toss a pair of shoes out their doors. When we travelled through on later convoys, the people were no longer pointing at their mouths; rather, they raised their legs and pointed at their feet!

In the deep, hard winter of 1994, while leading convoys to Zenica, my field officer and I often noticed one woman standing well away from the others with her two children at her side, bundled up against the bitter wind and freezing temperatures, too dignified to beg but still in need of anything that might come her way. Two weeks before Christmas, I put two good children's coats, boots, socks and gloves in a box and included a carton of Marlboro, a small bottle of French brandy, cheese, a small ham, a tin of sardines and two large bars of Swiss chocolate. On top of an iced Christmas cake in another box, I put 100 DM.

The next trip into Zenica, I slowed the convoy, then raced ahead; skidding to a stop, Ivan and I handed the startled woman the two boxes. We wished her a Merry Christmas, and off we roared, informing the convoy to follow.

★　★　★

CHAPTER 9

A Christmas Convoy

✦ ✦ ✦ ✦ ✦

Winter, 1994

The weather in the mountains of Bosnia in the winter of 1994 was extremely cold and snowy. The week before Christmas, I was again taking a large fourteen-truck convoy into Zenica, including a truck with medical supplies for delivery to war-ravaged Mostar.

From a Sitrep:

> *Small-arms fire was reported in Mostar and the Rastani Dam areas, nine explosions and one out-going artillery round near Vrapčići, two explosions in Baglai, four detonations in Mostar East, along with small-arms and HMG fire on the ARBiH/ BSA cease-fire line.*

73

After unloading the medical supplies in east Mostar, I instructed the driver to wait for our return in a couple of days. All my drivers were Croatian, so he was quite comfortable waiting on the Croatian side of town. The weather had been cold all week, and that day the snow was coming down heavily. Because of the war the snow was not being cleared, and the road out of Mostar was hard to distinguish from the fields on either side. I had my trusty Land Cruiser in four-wheel drive. The trucks were fully laden, weighing around sixteen tonnes each, with good tires and experienced drivers, so I decided not to make everyone chain up, not just yet.

From a Sitrep:

> *Jablanica/Prozor: Generally quiet. Exchanges of fire reported along the ARBiH/BSA confrontation line and in the area of Pazarić.*

Through Jablanica and then onto Prozor, we found plenty of packed snow on the road, giving pretty good grip, so still no reason to put on snow chains.

From a Sitrep:

> *Gornji Vakuf-Uskoplj: One mine explosion in the Santici area, two mine explosions and several bursts of small-arms fire reported in the town.*

Finally, just past the UN Britbat base at Gornji Vakuf-Uskoplj, I stopped the convoy. Over the VHF, I told each driver, "We will put on chains. When you get yours on, go and help the truck in front with theirs." No one responded to my message. This told me that they all thought chains were unnecessary. Since they were Croatian and I was not, they were just not going to chain up in this blizzard. I put on my coat and walked back down the line of trucks. In each truck, the chains were carried on the passenger side floor. At the first truck, I threw open the door; as the warm cab suddenly filled with a blizzard of snow, I grabbed the chains and threw them out onto the road, telling the driver, "Put on your chains!" I continued my act with the next four trucks until the drivers knew I was serious. I helped one of the newer guys before making my way back to the Cruiser. Bless Marko; he had woken from his slumber and had already chained up the Cruiser.

Nine of the trucks were six-by-four, sixteen-tonne Scanias, and fully loaded with chains on, they were good for almost any kind of winter weather. The three small ten-tonne Iveco four-by-four trucks, when chained up, were also good in the snow. The remaining truck was a six-by-six, ten-tonne Fiat driven by Damir. In most snow conditions it gave more traction than the others, so I decided not to chain up the Fiat.

★ ★ ★

By this time, with forty-five convoys under my belt, I knew each driver's strengths and weaknesses. It was sensible to put the fastest truck and driver in the rear and the slowest and less experienced at the front behind the most experienced driver, with the solid guys in the centre. If anything should happen to me, this most experienced driver would take over and lead the convoy to the nearest ICRC delegation or UN base, whichever was the closest.

The previous summer, young and novice driver Damir, on a similar convoy to Zenica, had crashed and flipped his truck. The ten-tonne Mercedes truck he was driving had a very small tank with not enough fuel to get to Zenica. Therefore, he had to carry a twenty-five-litre jerrycan of diesel in the cab. Each convoy, I would tell Damir to make sure the jerrycan was secure and was not going to skid around on the cab floor. Because he was still a little nervous and inexperienced, I had placed him second, behind the convoy leader.

That trip, I received a panicked call from the driver behind Damir; "Come back! Damir has crashed." Sure enough, the unsecured jerry-can had become jammed under the pedals. Damir couldn't get to the brakes fast enough, went off the road and ended upside down in a field. It only took me ten minutes to stop the convoy and race back; Damir was standing in the field by the roadside, arms outstretched euphorically, having climbed out through the broken window. I was equally relieved. The wheels had barely stopped spinning before a couple of locals had cans under the tank, siphoning out the precious diesel fuel.

Euphoric Damir and "diesel catchers", 1994

★   ★   ★

Back to the convoy to Zenica: putting snow chains on the Fiat was difficult because the wheels were close together, making it hard to connect them. After an hour spent getting all the trucks, except the Fiat, chained up and ready to go, we headed out on Route Gannett. The road was flat with loose gravel but well maintained by the UN. The River Bistrica, in full flood, followed the route for many kilometres. The snow was coming down as heavily as ever, and I could only see the first truck behind me. I was not worried because, as usual, we were in VHF radio contact. Damir was again following in number two position, behind the convoy leader. The road was now completely covered with at least fifteen centimetres of snow that was getting deeper by the minute. But I didn't know that the temperature was so low, ice was forming under the covering of snow.

We should be OK moving slowly, I thought, *And get into Zenica before dark.* Then I got a panicked call from Damir, who was yelling over the radio that he was almost in the river.

I instructed all the drivers to stop where they were and not pull over. The deep snow covered where the gravel road ended, and the ditch started. I didn't want anybody else getting stuck, or worse. I hurried back and saw Damir, white-faced in his truck; his vehicle was completely across the road with the front wheels perilously close to the fast-flowing river. He might have slipped in at any moment. After coaxing him out of his cab and down onto the road, I got him to start digging the rear wheels clear of snow in preparation to put on chains.

The Cheshire Regiment of the British Army, under the UN flag, maintained this section of the road. They had a base just outside of Gornji Vakuf-Uskoplj in a large industrial building by the name of the Precision Factory. A few kilometres past the base, I noticed, despite the blizzard, a British Army Armoured Personnel Carrier (APC) parked by the side of the track. I headed over, hoping to get the APC guys to pull the Fiat back onto the road, where we'd put on chains, and away we'd go.

I banged on the rear door of the APC; it swung open to reveal six soldiers in the back, sheltered from the blizzard, brewing up tea. I was still wet and cold from helping the drivers put on chains. The warmth and tea aroma wafting out made me wish I could change places with one of the soldiers for an hour – or until someone came along and sorted out my problem. That wasn't going to happen. *It's your convoy and your problem, so no tea for you, Roger!*

I explained that I really needed a tow.

"Of course."

They packed up the tea things and followed me the two kilometres back to where poor Damir was still digging, burdened with freezing snow. The driver nosed his APC close enough to the Fiat to allow another soldier to attach a sturdy towing cable, and then very slowly started to reverse. The APC's steel tracks were just turning, but there was no movement backwards at all. To the driver's horror, the twenty-tonne APC *and* the Fiat started to slide on the ice towards the river. The only thing to do was to immediately release the tow wire and hope both vehicles stopped their slide into the river. To everyone's huge relief, this did the trick. Without the weight of the truck, the APC driver easily reversed back up onto the road. I thanked him, and off he trundled into the snowstorm, likely to stop, brew some more tea and have a biscuit.

Things were not looking good, especially for me keeping my job; the Fiat had stopped sliding but was now even closer to the river. I was talking to Damir and wondering what to do next, when I noticed two British Army Officers standing a few yards away. They must have been monitoring what was going on with the APC. I couldn't grasp much of what was said, except I did hear one say to the other, surely for my benefit, "What kind of idiot would be running convoys without snow chains in this weather?"

All this time, Marko was trying to contact any of our delegations to inform them of the situation. Unfortunately, the VHF set was only good for a fifteen-kilometre range, even less when surrounded by hills. Also, the more powerful HF set did not seem to be working at all. Later, we discovered that the oil in the front-mounted antenna had congealed, interfering with the automatic tuning. Marko tried to raise the delegations across the whole of the former Yugoslavia. He even tried to call Geneva, to no avail.

The Route Gannet was one of the main supply routes into Central Bosnia, with regular convoys all day, every day. We had been blocking this route for four hours, and it was beginning to get dark when, to my dismay, a UN helicopter flew over, likely dispatched to determine what the holdup was. The pilot was either very good or very mad; he was so low, the wash from his rotors blew the snow down onto us poor frozen folk thirty metres below. He did two passes, then flew off. I was beginning to think that the only option was to push Damir's truck into the river and clear the road for all the other convoys. Later, I learned that there were ten convoys, around 100 trucks, patiently waiting behind us in the blizzard.

My bacon was seriously saved by the appearance of a Dutch UN heavy-recovery vehicle. With a minimum of fuss, a cable was hooked up and the Fiat was effortlessly pulled up onto the road. I thought about giving the Dutch soldiers a group hug but decided to help chain up the Fiat instead. Fifteen minutes later, we were once again rolling along towards Zenica. It was six o'clock and dark. The golden rule of running convoys in Central Bosnia was, *Do not drive at night!*

From a Sitrep:

> *Banditry is now a major problem in some areas. Do not travel at night, unless absolutely necessary.*

Almost no one drove at night for fear of bandits. Except Roger and his convoy, followed by another 100 or so trucks of many other NGOs. I was wondering how to put all this in my end-of-convoy report. Whichever way I worded it, the results were the same. I could also imagine what Maria would say in her weekly report to Geneva. None of these scenarios suggested I would be convoyer for too much longer, but I'd worry about that when we finally got back. In the meantime, I still had to get everyone and their loads to Zenica and Tuzla, and then safely back to Split.

We were still at least three hours away from Zenica. The snow had stopped falling, and a beautiful full moon shone high in the starry sky with the snow laying "deep and crisp and even...." With snow chains on, the Land Cruiser had no trouble ploughing a path for my trucks to follow; the other convoys would at least have a track to follow when they came along behind us through the white and silent landscape.

Passing through village after village, I could only see the occasional glimmer from an oil lamp behind the shuttered windows, but not a soul outside anywhere. The local people had endured three years of war and were simply trying to survive one more winter in the harsh and stone-cold landscape, waiting for spring and hoping for the war to end.

Marko managed to contact ICRC Zenica to let them know our position and that we should arrive before ten that night. There was just one more checkpoint at Busovača to pass through. The guards were hunkered down, trying to keep warm and probably enjoying a glass or two. So, I drove the Land Cruiser slowly through and waited just past the raised, frozen-in-place barrier for the rest of the convoy to pass. The road was now quite clear as the wind had blown most of the snow away. There was no more ice, so I called the drivers to remove their chains. Once more, I was met with radio silence. Removing snow chains was worse than putting them on because the snow had lots of time to turn to ice and seize everything solid.

By this time, we had been on the road for fourteen hours. All of us were tired and hungry. Before leaving on convoy, everyone packed some food and water as there were few, if any, places to buy anything. I would always take a bunch of bananas, a bag of mixed nuts and a bottle of water, enough to keep going for a couple of days.

* * *

Once, when held up waiting for a UN convoy to pass on a treacherous mountain track, a scruffy, shoeless little eight-year-old girl saw me eating a banana. Her eyes were like saucers as she uttered, "Banana!" I could do no more than to give her my remaining bunch.

* * *

But on this convoy, we all yearned for a hot dinner, not easy to find in Zenica in the winter. I knew, because of the late hour, we would be sleeping on empty stomachs. Beating off the accumulated ice and snow, Marko and I soon had my chains off and back in their bag. The drivers, realizing we would be there all night if necessary, climbed out of their cosy cabs. With shovels and tire irons, they knocked off the ice and threw the frozen chains back onto the passenger floor. Damir, nicely recovered from his near-death experience, also got his chains off in record time.

Two hours later, we approached the darkened city of Zenica. The city had very little electricity during most of the war, and even less during the winter months. The Soviet-style high-rise tenement blocks were all in darkness. I felt bad for the people living in those freezing apartments. There was no work, little food, no money and no heating except from a small, locally made steel stove – if one was lucky enough to find a bit of firewood. Many of the trees in the city had been cut down and burnt. There was nothing for the local citizens to look forward to except waiting out the war and then trying to rebuild their lives. Marko was gently snoring away, slowly slipping down onto the floor of the Land Cruiser. The drama was behind us; I hoped the next day would be easier.

Three hundred metres ahead, right in the middle of the road, my headlights picked up two people fighting. Quickly I radioed and stopped the convoy. Racing ahead, I saw a man run off, disappearing into the darkness, leaving a young girl on her knees in the snow, sobbing. The fifteen-year-old said she was going home to her mother when she was beaten up and robbed of the five DM that she had made by standing out in the freezing weather all day, selling a few packs of cigarettes. I had no money on me, but Marko did, and he gave her five DM. After a few moments, she straightened herself up, thanked us and limped off to her mum, who was waiting for her in their frigid, two-room apartment. On a freezing winter night in the middle of a Bosnian road, this poor girl had become a victim of war-induced desperation.

At ten thirty, we finally arrived at the ICRC warehouse near the centre of town. The local warehouse staff had offered to work late to refuel our vehicles, ready for an early start the following morning for the final leg of the convoy. Six trucks would be unloaded in Zenica; the remaining seven I would take onto Tuzla.

With all trucks safely in the hands of the Zenica staff, we drove across town in two Land Cruisers, to the old peoples' home that we used for accommodation. The ICRC rented a whole unoccupied wing from the local authorities. In theory, it was supposed to get two hours of electricity a day to enable the staff to cook and try to warm the place up for the elderly residents. I'd stayed there many times and had not noticed any electricity, at all. We each had a room, freezing cold, complete with damp bedding. The residents must really have suffered with the cold. I had a banana leftover from the day, and that was my dinner, washed down with a hot, yes hot, cup of black tea. I had my little gas camping stove, a small saucepan, cup and tea bags with me at all times, perfect for evenings like that. I jotted down what happened that day, and at 11:30, fully clothed, I was fast asleep.

My small travel alarm jolted me awake, still freezing, at 5 a.m. In the cold, dark cafeteria, we wordlessly sat down to our cold salami sandwich and even colder coffee. The nursing home staff made the breakfast and coffee when they had electricity and left it out in the canteen for any convoy personnel passing through. It beat having no breakfast, but only just.

The trucks and my Cruiser were refuelled and ready for our six o'clock start. It had snowed again during the night, so we put the snow chains back on. The drivers were not happy but realized we really did need to fit chains when I asked. No one wanted a repeat of the previous day, especially me. It was just three days before

Christmas, and we wanted to be back in Split as soon as possible. Route Skoda towards Tuzla was in pretty good condition; as long as we kept chains on, everything should be fine. There was just one army checkpoint from Zenica to Tuzla because we were in Army of the Republic of Bosnia and Herzegovina (ARBiH) territory. However, there were two UN posts, south at Ribnica and north alongside a small ARBiH army post, five kilometres farther on. Route Skoda took us through Visoko.

From a Sitrep:

> *The BSA have placed mines near their checkpoint at the Visoko Bridge. These mines can be detonated electronically, and radio transmission in the vicinity of the bridge is prohibited. Vares (nine artillery/mortar rounds). Olovo (thirty-one detonations and LMG fire). Around 125 detonations and sporadic bursts of small arms fire reported in the Dastansko area. The Olovo area suffered a decrease in the shelling where approximately 268 detonations were registered. In the area of Kladanj a few explosions were reported. With fifty-three detonations heard in the Ribnica area.*

The route followed the River Krivaja and was exposed to the BSA forces' front line for five kilometres. The UN stopped all convoys at the Ribnica checkpoint and insisted, because of the real danger of being fired on from just across the river, on escorting them through this section with an APC in front and one behind. All UN and NGO convoys travelling this route, "The Ribnica Shooting Gallery", had to accept the escort. Except, of course, the ICRC.

I slowed down and stopped at the UN barrier. My seven drivers knew the procedure and pulled over to wait for me. I spoke with the UN Norwegian captain, emphasizing that the ICRC could not have an armed escort. He understood, but his orders were not to let any unescorted convoys past this point. I insisted that we would proceed unescorted; after a radio call to his Norbat headquarters in Tuzla, we were waved through.

Everyone removed their snow chains during my chat with the captain. The road was clear, and we could move faster without chains. We had collected bulletproof jackets from ICRC Zenica the previous night. Before leading the convoy out, I walked back down the line of trucks and looked at each driver to make sure they had donned their jacket and helmet. The jacket, complete with all the ballistic plates, weighed twenty kilograms; it was uncomfortable and made driving difficult. This was why I always checked. The bullet-proofs would be handed in on our way back through Zenica.

I had the slowest truck in the number one position behind me, and the fastest bringing up the rear. Each truck was spaced at fifty metres, with me 500 metres ahead. We went as fast as the slowest truck; two kilometres in, we passed the burnt-out remains of a Belgian six-truck convoy that had been attacked with mortars and heavy machine-gun fire one year previously. We did not stop until the road turned right and away from the BSA positions just over the river. The danger was genuine; this section took a relatively short time, then we could stop and remove our jackets and helmets. It was a long thirty-five minutes. My biggest worry was having a truck break down along this dangerous stretch. *What would I do if we broke down?* I didn't know, but I would figure something out.

At the ARBiH post, we stopped and regrouped before the last leg to Tuzla. An old Second World War Soviet T-34 main battle tank sat with the turret and main gun pointing down the road towards the BSA positions. This hulking throwback must have been blown up a few times in its fifty-one-year career. The turret was almost completely covered in large, crudely cut welded steel plates, and the body was draped in thick, heavy sheets of black rubber; I presumed to protect it from small-arms fire. It was not a machine for today's war, but it sure looked menacing. The ARBiH had always struggled to arm themselves, so anything, including this brooding museum piece, helped continue the fight. In contrast, the Serbian Army, which supported the BSA and the ARSK, had the majority of the JNA army equipment. The Croatians had some of this hardware, but it was a fraction of what the JNA had. And the Muslims (ARBiH), who were under a UN arms embargo, had to make war with whatever they could smuggle in, capture or cobble together.

T-34 at north end – Ribnica Shooting Gallery, 1994
(Courtesy of commons.wikimedia.org)

★ ★ ★

On one previous trip, we were held up at the same checkpoint, waiting for the military to move the T-34 (why it was across the road I had no idea), when I noticed a young Muslim girl, no more than seven or eight years old, walking towards us and speaking to my drivers. As she passed, I caught her eye and asked what she had for sale.

"My grandfather asked me to sell his WWII bayonet."

"How much?"

Without a pause, she shyly said, "thirty Deutschmark?" I was happy to give her forty to see her run off home and tell her story.

★ ★ ★

It was bitterly cold, but thankfully the snow was holding off. Leaving the river and the ARBiH post behind, we continued on to Tuzla. We seemed to be the only people on the road, perhaps because of the cold, or there might have been an incident about which we had not been informed. It had been three days since I attended a UN security briefing; a lot could change in three hours, never mind three days. Marko managed to make radio contact just after Ribnica, letting ICRC Tuzla know where we were and our next point of contact. We had no reports of any trouble on our route, but the lack of vehicles seemed a bit unusual. Perhaps the other NGOs had planned their convoys to be finished before Christmas? The remainder of the trip to Tuzla was free of any drama.

I was looking forward to sleeping in the relatively modern Hotel Bristol that night. It had electricity and hot water. And there were a few basement bars open where the famous burek, a Bosnian meat pie, could be found. After a whole banana and a cold salami sandwich in the last eighteen hours, I was ready for dinner.

From a Sitrep:

Tuzla: Two mortar and two artillery impacts in the city.

It was five and dark. The BSA had just started the evening's ritual of random shelling, just three or four rounds, but enough to wear down everyone in the city a little more. The cost of these projectiles and the effort to load the big guns, then listen to the bang, must have been quite wearing on the BSA artillerymen, stuck in their damp hilltop bunkers, twenty kilometres away. During this cold

Christmas, no one could know that in a mere five months' time, all this effort and expenditure would pay off one gruesome evening in late May, claiming the lives of seventy-one young people.

At the warehouse, we left the trucks to be unloaded and refuelled for the next day. The drivers jammed into the back of my Cruiser, and I dropped them off, along with Marko, at the Hotel Bristol. I continued to the delegation where, in the radio room, I wrote out my field trip form for the next day's return journey to Zenica. Everyone had by this time finished for the day and gone home, but the radio room was manned twenty-four hours in case of an emergency.

In the previous week, the front of the Hotel Bristol had been hit by two rockets, so our assigned rooms were at the rear of the hotel and were less likely to suffer any damage should the gentlemen decide to fire a few more. I was so hungry, dirty and tired that I really didn't care where my room was. Behind the thick black-out curtains, I turned on the bright electric lights and had the world's best hot shower before meeting Marko in the basement bar, where I ate a large burek and downed a couple of bottles of local beer. A blissful two hours of relaxation and civil conversation. Just starting to really relax, I was standing outside the hotel on the street, getting some air. I hadn't noticed a policeman standing just behind me until, without warning, he shot off a full magazine from his assault rifle into the air, once again spiking my adrenaline levels.

Christmas Eve

During the summer months, the trip from Tuzla through Zenica to Split took fifteen hours, but it obviously took longer in the winter. I would try my best to get everyone back before the holiday. It was six in the morning and still dark when we started to leave Tuzla. The next stop was Zenica, where we would collect the six drivers left behind the previous day. The road conditions were good, with no ice and just a dusting of snow. Marko managed to stay awake for the first two hours until we passed through the UN North Post at Ribnica, unescorted, of course. Everyone had donned their bulletproof jackets, and their helmets were strapped on tight. Without the chinstrap properly fastened and adjusted, the helmet would give about the same degree of protection as a thick book balanced on top of our heads. Both would fly off easily in the event of a sudden security incident. So, with all trucks spaced out fifty metres, and Marko and I well ahead, off we went.

Maybe the gunners across the river had had a bit too much Christmas cheer the previous night and were still tucked up in their beds, sleeping off hangovers. Or maybe they were up and about early, perhaps thinking they should try to bag another convoy before the end of the year. One never knew which way it would go. Safely at the other end of the shooting gallery, we pulled over. The guys were happy to get the jackets and helmets off. It was always a tense thirty-five minutes, more so for the truck drivers. Damir, driving the slowest truck, would be the perfect target for a well-aimed 100-millimetre high-explosive tank round, which would bring the whole convoy to a halt, leaving everyone sitting ducks.

The remainder of the morning was plain sailing; it was beginning to look like we would make it into Croatian territory that day. I then received a radio message from ICRC Zenica, informing me of a security incident at the Turbe checkpoint. We were not actually driving through Turbe but passing within two kilometres and were close enough to risk becoming involved with the incident. Details of the incident were not broadcast via the radio as all sides of the conflict listened to the transmissions. To be informed of a security risk ahead was enough. I could then decide on the best course of action.

Then to my dismay, I was asked to divert to Vogošća and collect three ICRC delegates and take them to Split. The town is right on the front line, very close to the Bosnian and Herzegovinian capital, Sarajevo, which had been under siege almost since the war began. The three delegates, one with the German and the other two with the Danish Red Cross, had finished a gruelling four-month tour in Sarajevo and were heading home in time for Christmas. This was not looking good for the convoy's plan to be in Split at the end of the day, but never mind: these guys wanted to get home too.

From a Sitrep:

> Sarajevo: Levels of activity decreased with only 724 firing incidents. There were twelve military and civilian casualties. The airhead remained open; an anti-sniping team was engaged by a single small-arms round. The BSA and ARBiH exchanged tank artillery and mortar fire in the Ilijaš area. Fighter aircraft were moved into the Maglai area to monitor the fighting between the BSA and ARBiH.

I radioed back to ICRC Zenica and asked them to send the six Split trucks to the UN Britbat base at Vitez, where the seven other Split trucks would meet them and wait for me. There was plenty of secure parking at the base. I could divert to Vogošća, pick up my delegates, return to Vitez and then continue with the whole convoy to Split.

I asked Marko to stay awake because the café where the three delegates were waiting for us was in an area often shelled and mortared. I had been there twice previously, and both times had felt very uneasy. It felt like a real Wild-West town, so the quicker we got in, got our guys and headed away, the better. The café was packed full of soldiers and civilians, drinking and trying to warm up. The weather was cold but sunny. My three passengers were waiting outside, frozen to the bone. The atmosphere inside these cafés and bars could be quite intimidating when full of soldiers, get-rich-quick businessmen, people smugglers (there was a thriving business smuggling those who could pay, out of Sarajevo) and black marketeers. This was definitely not a town coffee shop where one would pop in and have a slice of carrot cake and a large cappuccino on a Saturday morning after shopping for new shoes.

The three delegates each had two large hold-all bags and a small rucksack. The German guy, whom I would not forget in a hurry, was also carrying two plastic shopping bags. I already had three sacks of diplomatic mail, my and Marko's overnight bags, plus the equipment we normally carried, including our two monstrously heavy bulletproof jackets and helmets. The Land Cruiser was full. I decided that when we met up with the convoy waiting in Vitez, I would distribute the three delegates into a truck each, which would provide more room for them, and I thought the drivers would appreciate a bit of company.

Two hours later, we arrived in Vitez. Because time was short, I had Marko radio the convoy leader and ask him to have all the drivers back in their trucks and ready to go when we turned up. One of the Danish guys plus luggage I put in with Ivan; the other Dane was travelling with Eldin; and the German guy, Hans, I put in with Anur. During the two-hour trip from Vogošća to Vitez, Hans constantly complained about everything, especially how he "needed to be home for Christmas!" Anur could be very moody, and by the end of the day, he was ready to kill me for saddling him with Hans. Anur could speak no English, and I presumed Hans could speak no Serbo-Croat. *Problem solved,* I thought, except I forgot about the VHF radio in Anur's truck.

Another driver reported he had a BRC delegate, Ann, from Zenica in his cab, also getting a lift with the convoy on her way home to England. As she was the only woman on the convoy and someone I could talk to when Marko resumed sleeping, I asked if she would like to travel with us in the Cruiser. She was happy to sit in the back and be bounced around with the mail and luggage for the rest of the trip to Split.

From a Sitrep:

> *Turbe: There has been heavy and continuous shelling in this area.*

I still didn't know what the security incident was about, but we did need to avoid the Turbe area. I decided to take the Bugojno road on the way to Gornji Vakuf-Uskoplj.

From a Sitrep:

> *Bugojno: Four days of fierce street fighting between the ARBiH and the HVO, leave one hundred and ninety-eight dead and three hundred and forty-one wounded.*

We had been travelling for no more than an hour when ICRC Zenica called to inform us that the road was blocked by a group of armed civilians just outside of the town of Bugojno, and to please wait. We would be updated when further information was available. I found a wide stretch of road and halted the convoy, reminding everyone not to pull off the road because of the landmine risk. I informed my passengers of the situation and that we would move as soon as it was safe.

Dear Hans, who by this time had consumed half the contents of one plastic shopping - twelve cans of beer, and some of the contents of the other plastic shopping bag full of bananas (where he got bananas from in Sarajevo was beyond me), had commandeered Anur's VHF radio and was constantly asking me when we were going to move because, "I need to be home for Christmas!"

The radios all vehicles were equipped with were only to be used briefly for convoy business. Hans had no authority even to touch the radio. When he took a breath, I quickly told him to please stay off the radio as I needed to keep the channel clear in case of an emergency. We had been waiting for over an hour and still no word from Zenica, but plenty of words from complaining Hans. Eventually, I walked back to Anur's truck, climbed into the cab and, elbowing a surprised Hans aside, unscrewed the mic jack plug. I then handed a smiling Anur my own hand-held VHF radio, telling him to keep it in the door pocket away from his passenger. I could not allow anyone to jeopardize the convoy's safety, ICRC delegate or not.

It was frustrating waiting, especially as Hans so needed to be home, but clearance from Zenica was essential to proceed through Bugojno. At 3 p.m., the radio crackled to life, "377 the Bugojno road is now clear and safe to travel. Repeat, the road is now clear and safe to travel, over."

"Thank you, Zenica. Leaving now. Next radio contact Prozor, over."

"Well copied, 377. Merry Christmas. Over and out."

Finally, we were able to continue. Marko had been fast asleep during the last two hours but woke with a start when Zenica called, giving us the go-ahead.

There was no way we could get to Split that night. On a good day, on dry summer roads, the trip from Vitez to Split was at least seven hours. Getting there now would mean travelling in the dark, and I was not going to do that. It was simply too dangerous. So, the only option was to spend the night in the small ICRC office in Jablanica. We should arrive there just before dark. I hoped the UN Malbat would have enough room to park our thirteen trucks in their compound. Their base was in an abandoned shoe factory with a large, secure parking area at the rear.

Through Bugojno, we didn't see any evidence of the civilian road-block. We went on to Prozor, not forgetting to let ICRC Zenica know our plan. Next contact, Jablanica. I was happy with the road conditions; it was freezing and too cold for snow, and there was no ice, which meant the nasty snow chains could stay on the cab floor and gently rust away.

At last: we arrived in Jablanica, the town that Marshall Tito, the partisan leader fighting Nazi rule, escaped to when being pursued by the German army. At one time, there was a railway bridge across the Neretva River at Jablanica. Tito just had time to get across in the steam train he was travelling in, then blow up the bridge and leave his pursuers frustrated on the other side of the gorge. The train is still there, exactly where it came to a halt all those years ago. Tito, whose proper name was Josip Broz, became the Yugoslav Prime Minister from 1944 to 1963. He then became President for Life until his death in 1980, which started the chain of events leading to the breakup of Yugoslavia.

The Malaysians at the UN Malbat were surprised to see me turn up with thirteen trucks but arranged for our convoy to park overnight in their muddy compound. I took ten people to the ICRC office, then went back for the other eight, including a most unhappy Hans, who would not accept a lift to the office, insisting that I personally drive him on to Split that night. "Everyone can make their own way in the morning," he graciously allowed. As I firmly disabused him of this notion, red-faced, fuming Hans then walked the two kilometres to the office through deep, wet slush, mud and snow.

Luckily, there was a restaurant open in the town, and we enjoyed a good hot meal before heading back to where we would sleep, on the office floor. The office had just two small rooms and we jammed in together, head to toe, in one of the rooms. The two Danish guys, Hans, and Ann were not expecting to spend a night out, so didn't have sleeping bags. The local head of office found a blanket for each of them, and we settled down. With nineteen unwashed bodies jammed together, and the temperature just above freezing, it was a rather uncomfortable night.

Christmas Day

Overnight, the weather had turned colder, but it was still clear and luckily too cold for snow. By 6 a.m. I had delivered everyone back to the trucks. A now-subdued Hans once again sat in with Anur, and we headed out on the last leg to Split. Fifteen kilometres before Mostar, on the north side of the Koviljača road tunnel, I stopped the convoy and told everyone to put on flak jackets and helmets. My drivers still had Zenica's bullet-proofs, as we'd had no time the day before to call in and drop them off, but the much more lightweight flak jackets were enough in this area. The road south of the tunnel was under Serb artillery observation and subject to occasional shelling, so walking back down the convoy, I checked that everyone, including my delegate passengers, had complied and put on helmets and flak jackets. I entered into an annoying battle of wits with one of the Danish delegates, who was stubbornly refusing to put on a flak jacket. I stared him down and waited him out. He succumbed when he knew we would not be leaving until he donned his. With Damir in second place and each truck spaced at the regulation fifty metres, I was already through the tunnel when I called the convoy through.

The road was flat and straight until Mostar. I had travelled along there many times, but the feeling of vulnerability still weighed like a stone in the pit of my stomach. Being under the gaze of the artillerymen, dug in up in the hills on both sides of the road, and wondering if we would be targeted, was no fun. On the first day of the convoy, just outside Mostar, I noticed two new shell craters in the road, so I knew the gunners had the precise coordinates to hit the road that we were at that moment travelling on.

We drove for five minutes, then ten, then fifteen. Twenty minutes and we were still trundling along at fifty kilometres an hour, totally exposed, in full view of the gunners. I was thinking, *We'll will be lucky and not be fired on; it's Christmas Day, after all.* Then, ten metres away, just off to my left, I saw an eruption of black soil. There was no sound, just this plume of soil falling back to earth. Christmas be dammed! The Serbs were targeting us as we drove along, maybe just letting us know they were there, or signalling a Christmas greeting. Luckily, the soft dirt absorbed all the blast and shrapnel. It would have been lethal had the shell impacted on the road just ten metres away. But it didn't, and as far as I could tell, there was only one shell fired.

Marko, who was actually awake, called ICRC Mostar and advised them of the event and that we would enter Mostar in twenty minutes to collect the truck and driver we had left there three days previously.

Just outside of town, we removed helmets and jackets. I suspected a few of the guys had already removed theirs back up the road. With the final truck reconnected to the convoy, we made our way past the sprawling, totally ruined former Yugoslav air force base and headed toward the Bosnian-Croatian border at Metković. Through the border, once on the Croatian side, we stopped at a large truck stop and had our first Croatian coffee in four days. It was delicious.

After a hurried breakfast, we were on the road again, with everyone keen to keep moving and get home. I asked Marko to contact ICRC Split and arrange flights for my four delegates. The Welcome Desk radioed back and told me that a driver would meet us at the warehouse to take the passengers on to the airport. The rest of the trip back up the coast road towards Split was uneventful – a blessing given all that had happened during the last few days. We soon arrived at the ICRC warehouse. My three pleasant and one unpleasant passenger sat in the delegation Land Cruiser, waiting to leave for the half-hour trip to the airport. I wished them all a Merry Christmas. The Danes thanked me, Hans muttered something and Ann congratulated me on my patience.

Working in these situations was not easy, and even the relaxed and jovial times had undercurrents of tension. The stress was palpable, and although I knew that Hans likely had a tough mission and was having trouble dealing with the turmoil of his emotions, his privilege and sullenness didn't make it easier on the rest of the crew. It was clear this work wasn't for everyone. Some suffered more than others; a few showed the effects more than others.

Those of my drivers who had cars offered to take the vehicle-less drivers home, which allowed me to go straight to the delegation and write my report. This had been my seventy-sixth convoy.

CHAPTER 10

Roma

* * * * *

Christmas Day, 1994, 6 p.m.

I sat at a borrowed desk, trying to finish my convoy report. Writing a report was the last thing I wanted to do at the best of times and doing this one was no fun at all. I had just left the finished document on Maria's desk when she called on my VHF radio, inviting me to come and spend the evening with she and her husband. We had a pleasant time: good food, good Croatian wine and good conversation, just what I needed after this last convoy. By eleven o'clock, I was beginning to wilt; I headed back to my apartment and was asleep before my head hit the pillow.

December 26ᵗʰ

No work today; I had time to do my laundry and sit and read a book, then maybe cook some dinner (i.e., warm up a ration pack), or maybe not, *I might pick up a pizza*. I would attend the security briefing the next day at the UN, then prepare for a one-truck convoy to the Tarčin Prison Camp.

December 28ᵗʰ

My alarm jolted me awake at 4:30 a.m.; all I wanted to do was stay in bed on this December day. We left Split with one truck loaded with individual food parcels destined for the Tarčin Prison Camp known as "The Silos", named after the large window-less grain silo where up to 600 inmates were detained. The ICRC gained access to the camp for the first time in November 1992. The guards clearly resented our presence. Thin, gaunt, dirty prisoners were marched out under their baleful looks; the guards carried clubs or wicked-looking whips. During the two hours it took the prisoners to unload the truck, not one raised their eyes.

Sitting in the Cruiser, I was doing some paperwork when an English voice called to me from behind some wire netting over a window. He was a Muslim fighter and asked me if I could get him released. This request was, of course, totally out of my realm of responsibility.

Later, the senior Swiss delegate said the conditions had improved since his last visit when many prisoners were dying of starvation, thirst and daily beatings. There were also reports of inmates digging trenches on the front lines; exposed to gunfire, they were often injured or killed. Although it was known that the food would not get to the inmates, he said, "We should count this as a victory, by just having our presence here."

After the war, the prison commander and some of the guards were tried at the Hague Tribunal for crimes against humanity and received long prison sentences. Another small victory. In Bosnia alone, there were an additional 670 similar camps.

At the UN briefing the next day, I was informed there had been eleven artillery impacts on the Ribnica road on December 26th. We had passed through there just two days previously, encountering no issues.

From a Sitrep:

> Very heavy fighting on Mount Igman, situation there extremely tense. BSA forces discovered sixteen male BSA soldiers and four female BSA nurses killed and mutilated. The ARBiH reportedly to blame. Caution still required north of Mostar on route Gannet due to the road being regularly shelled.

January to August 1995

I escorted another thirty-eight convoys into Central Bosnia, 114 to date.

One evening in mid-May, I arrived back at our warehouse after another long and dusty but otherwise uneventful Zenica/Tuzla convoy. Waiting for everyone to get organized for lifts home while they were standing around chatting and smoking, I checked we were all present and accounted for. Each of us were somewhat tired and dishevelled, but there was one guy with his back to me, looking especially messy, whom I didn't recognize. Something told me to try some mental arithmetic, never my strong point:

14 trucks, each truck having one driver = 14 people

1 Land Cruiser, myself and my field officer = 2 people

After several attempts, I figured out there should be sixteen people standing around. I counted once more; the total came to seventeen.

This was one person too many. I tapped the extra-dishevelled person on the shoulder, "What are you doing here?"

"I came from Zenica in the back of one of the trucks," he nervously replied.

Oddly enough, not one of my drivers seemed to have a clue who this guy was. This was really serious: a stowaway on a Red Cross convoy, crossing numerous borders and checkpoints. It was rare to be checked on the return journey as the trucks were empty, but it did sometimes happen. If the guy had been discovered, the whole ICRC relief operation would have been compromised. Never mind what would likely have been the fate of the poor guy. The drivers were all quiet, waiting to see what I would do. I moved closer, reached out, shook his hand and said, "Welcome to Split." Winning the lottery would not have made him, or my drivers, happier.

"Best not mention this to anyone," I said to my field officer.

One month later, I was asked to do a similar thing; there was no doubt what I would do.

★ ★ ★

When we ran convoys anywhere in the former Yugoslavia, we were in radio contact with each delegation en route. I knew all the radio operators well, not only talking to them on convoy but also submitting the mandatory field trip form before each trip. They were all great, dedicated people. One evening while I sat in the Zenica radio room chatting to Mirko, he seemed unusually nervous. Eventually, he told me his predicament.

Three years earlier, his wife and two small children had managed to leave Zenica on one of the last bus trips from Central Bosnia to the Adriatic coast. The trip was dangerous; during the journey, the bus was stopped many times by local militia looking for men of fighting age, who were dragged off and taken away. No one knew where they were taken to, and everyone was too terrified to ask. The women and older folk were robbed each time the bus was stopped until they had no valuables left. Eventually, the remaining passengers reached Croatian territory. In Split, Mirko's wife and children got on another bus heading north. After four days of constant travel, they made it to Germany and safety, where they applied for asylum and refugee status.

Over the previous three years, Mirko had received only two letters from them. "I have been working here for the ICRC since that time. I cannot wait any longer, Roger. I must try and get to Germany. Will you help me?"

After listening to his story, I could do no more than say, "Of course, my friend. How can we do this?" Later in the bar, after the end of his shift, we came up with a simple plan.

The plan was this: the next day, early, he would phone the delegation and say he was sick and would not be in to work. This would ensure the relief radio operator would be in and that radio coverage would continue. He would pack one small rucksack and nothing else. I would let my field officer in on the plan and ask him to ride with one of the truck drivers as a passenger. Mirko would then look and act as my field officer on the trip back to Split.

"Wait at the end of the last bridge out of town, and I will make sure I am far enough ahead of the convoy to stop for you to jump into the passenger seat. Jump in fast, Mirko!"

Early the following morning, when it was still dark, the last truck driver reported to me that he had left the warehouse and was bringing up the rear. Quickly copying this, I sped across the bridge to where I had arranged to meet Mirko. As I neared the other side, my headlights on main beam, he was nowhere in sight. The convoy would be right behind me in another two minutes, and then everyone would figure out what was going on. I trusted all these guys, but sometimes the less everyone knew, the better. Just as the headlights of the lead truck appeared around the corner, a breathless Mirko wrenched open the door and threw himself in. I'm sure my heart was pounding as wildly as his.

After catching his breath, he explained, "On my way to meet you, I was stopped by a police curfew patrol and asked where I was going this early in the morning." With nerves of steel, he nonchalantly produced his ICRC pass and said, "To the delegation to start my shift." Satisfied, the police handed his pass back, wished him a good day and walked off. At the first corner, he ran faster than he had ever run, hoping to put enough distance between himself and the patrol before they realized he was walking *away* from the delegation, not towards it!

There was little worry having him in the Land Cruiser; he was an ICRC employee, so exempt from military duty, and he held an ICRC pass. The only risk for him was travelling through Croatia en route to Germany without a passport. Knowing him, I thought he would have had a good story for the border guards to explain why he was travelling on an ICRC pass. *And for me?* If our exploit was discovered, I would likely have been sent home immediately. But I felt helping him reunite with his family was worth the risk.

We had no issues on the return leg, and as the trucks headed to the warehouse, I detoured and left Mirko at my apartment. I told him he could stay with me for as long as he needed to arrange the next leg of his journey. "Make yourself at home and help yourself to anything." I was up and out early the next morning, leaving him sleeping on the couch. At the delegation, everything was as normal, and no one had any idea the radio operator from ICRC Zenica was holed up in my apartment. But I was wondering how he was going to get out of Croatia, cross into Slovenia, then Austria, before crossing the last border into Germany.

That evening, sitting around the dining table Mirko, explained his plan. "Simple really," he said. "Today, I bought a ticket for a bus leaving first thing in the morning that will take me right through into Austria. Then it's just a matter of crossing into Germany."

As he laid out his plan, I thought to myself that if his ICRC pass was not accepted at each border, it was very likely he would be arrested and held in a detention centre somewhere, or possibly sent back to Bosnia.

Early the following morning, I dropped him off at the busy Split bus station, wished him good luck and, in a moment, he was swallowed up in the crowd. It seemed everyone there, coming or going, carried several large bags bursting at the seams with personal belongings. All were in a hurry to start their journeys to who knew where, anywhere I suspected, as long as it was away from the fighting.

I had a rare day off and decided to head home, have a coffee, make a sandwich, sit out on my balcony and enjoy the warm breeze coming off the Adriatic. When I opened the fridge to look for the milk, it was completely empty. Mirko had literally taken me up on my "help yourself to anything". He had consumed everything in the fridge, including a large block of Croatian cheese. I was about to get cross but realized the poor guy probably had not seen this amount of cheese in a few years.

A few months later, I received a postcard from him, from the West Edmonton Mall, where I knew there was plenty of delicious Canadian cheese!

★　★　★

As convoyer, I had full responsibility for the convoy, speed, safety, and security. The long hours and stress were beginning to wear me down. Little by little, I felt I was becoming less alert, taking risks I would not have dared three months before. For several months I had been asking the delegation for a break and some time away, only to be told I could not be spared due to the workload. Also, as one of only three expat convoyers left in the country, there was simply no one to replace me.

Then, one sunny, cold March morning while I sat in the delegation writing out yet another end-of-convoy report, our Welcome Desk staff member, Jenny, walked over and said, "ICRC Belgrade are quiet at the moment, so their convoyer has agreed to come to Split and take over from you for a week. Where would you like to go for your week off, Roger?"

Italy was just across the Adriatic, and I had never been to Rome.

"Rome. I would like to go to Rome, please Jenny."

One hour later, smiling and with a flourish, she handed me my flight tickets. "A driver will take you to the airport tomorrow morning. Your flight leaves at ten thirty. Have a good rest, Roger, and we'll see you next week."

With my small bag packed and 1,000 DM stuffed into my wallet, making sure I had a credit card in another pocket, I was happy to be getting away.

I wandered around Rome's Fiumicino airport in a daze, walking in the same direction as everybody else. All were moving fast, some running, talking on their phones. Everyone was dragging along far too much luggage. Not me, though; the river of humanity flowed both sides of me in a hurry to get somewhere important. The next thing I knew, I was on my knees, having just been catapulted across the walkway by an electric buggy. The driver stopped and was so apologetic, "Please forgive me," he pleaded. It was an accident, and as far as I could tell, nothing on the buggy was broken.

"Everything is just fine," I assured him.

I limped off to the airport bus terminal where I caught a crowded bus to the city centre. I had no plan; all I wanted to do was to find some accommodation, crawl into bed and sleep for the entire week. Not far from the centre, I checked into a youth hostel. My first mistake. That night, the noise coming through the thin walls from the other guests partying made sleep almost impossible. *Don't they know there's a war going on only 480 kilometres away?* So, the next morning, I decided to find a quieter place.

The sun was shining on my second day. Second mistake pending. With my bag over my shoulder, one hand in my pocket holding onto my stuffed wallet, I was again wandering aimlessly. I figured some accommodation would appear if I walked far enough. Suddenly, three Romany women, each with a screaming baby on her back, approached me and herded me into an alley. I woke up enough to realize I was getting robbed. Before I could react, they vanished as quickly as they appeared. Not a trace of them. Gone. So was my wallet.

Discovering this little fact made me quite cross. I walked on, fully alert now and trying not to look like a recently robbed tourist, I found a small hotel. Luckily, there was a vacancy. Pulling my credit card out of my other pocket I paid for five days in advance; I was very happy to find the windows had heavy drapes. I pulled them shut, delighted that not a chink of light from the street could enter and disturb my slumbers.

The large bruise on my hip from the airport cart incident produced an interesting gait; each day, as I limped across the city, I kept alert for my assailants. My fantasy was to wrestle them to the ground, babies included, hog-tie them with the 100 metres of Class A Alpine mountaineering rope that I always carried, then march all six into the nearest Carabinieri station and retrieve my wallet, complete with cash. A ridiculous plan and, of course, I carried no such rope. At the stroke of 6 p.m., I would head back to my tomb-like room, sleep for fourteen hours, wake up and go wandering again. I don't remember eating or drinking anything during this "rest".

On my last day, I decided to visit the Coliseum, where I found a quiet corner and, in the sun, sat and read a book. By sheer luck, I managed to catch the correct bus and was soon at the airport, carefully avoiding the silent-running electric buggies. An hour later, I woke up when the Croatian Airlines Boeing landed with a bump and squeal of tires. I felt good, relaxed, refreshed and ready for more convoys.

Things were heating up as the attacks were escalating. At this time, East Krajina was experiencing increasing levels of activity. I wondered if the north, west and south would be next.

From a Sitrep:

May 1995: Zagreb hit with aviation cluster bombs fired from the Serbian republic of Krajina, killing seven and injuring over 200.

I had other responsibilities in addition to my convoyer duties. I would chauffeur delegates into their new posts and take them out when their mission was over or they needed a break. I gave driving lessons to newly hired staff and driving tests to delegates who would be driving Land Cruisers and Corollas in their new posts. I did many things, but one responsibility stayed with me from the beginning, and that was truck driving.

As an expat, I was responsible for taking supplies into areas where our local staff could not travel. I was the only expat driver in the Split delegation, so whenever there were relief supplies needed in South Krajina, I was the person to go. Clearly, our Croatian drivers could not pass into the Serb-held enclave.

Five months after my *Roman Holiday*, I went to Knin and fell in love.

CHAPTER II

Oluja

● ● ● ● ●

August 1, 1995

Our head of relief at ICRC Split had received a message from ICRC Knin, Sector South, asking for an expatriate driver to be deployed there as a matter of urgency; the ARSK had drafted the local truck driver. He asked me if I would be willing to go and help out for a few days.

The ICRC had an understanding with the authorities that local Red Cross staff were exempt from being called up to serve in the military. But for the past month, the Croatian Army had been steadily advancing along the Dinaric Alps to the east of the Krajinas close to the main town of Knin, threatening the whole of the Serb-controlled area. The Krajinas consisted of four sectors – East, West, North and South: a crescent of land covering an area of 17,000-square kilometres, beginning at Pakrac in the northeast, across to Karlovac in the northwest and curving down to Knin in the south. The Krajinas were home to over 200,000 people. It seemed that the ARSK were drafting as many men of military age as possible in anticipation of a large-scale attack.

With over 114 convoys under my belt, I thought this change would be good. I had a month or so left of what was my fourth mission before returning to the UK, so I said, "Yes" to Knin. On my way to my apartment to pack, I stopped and bought a few things, including toothpaste, not forgetting some fruit, chocolate and a local newspaper for the delegation staff. Anything I brought was appreciated, as everything was in short supply due to the embargo on Serbia who backed and sustained the regime in the Krajinas.

Two weeks previously, during a trip into Sector South to deliver a truckload of medical goods, the local ICRC truck driver, before he was drafted into the army, asked me if I would be able to bring in a twenty-five-litre jerrycan of fuel for him. I agreed, as a jerrycan in the passenger side of my truck would not be questioned at the checkpoints. When I handed it over, he thanked me and said this fuel would be enough to get his family to safety in the event of the Croatian Army invading. I was surprised when he reached into his pocket and pulled out a Belgian-made Nagant gas-sealed pistol to give to me in payment. I would have loved to accept it as a souvenir but could not, due to the Red Cross "no weapons rule".

On the same trip, I brought in an expensive VCR for a staff member; he wanted it as a wedding gift to give to his brother. It was seen by the checkpoint soldiers in my truck, but they just shrugged when I said it was part of our relief supplies.

In May 1995, when delivering a truck with a load of medical supplies, I met the new medical delegate, who was waiting at the ICRC Knin warehouse to receive them. Standing with clipboard in hand, she was tall, blonde and elegant. The local warehouse staff began to unload the truck and, trying to regain my composure at meeting her, I noticed I had a puncture. As I started to remove the wheel, a dirty and heavy job, she came over, knelt beside me, and asked, "Can I lend you a hand?"

South, North, East and West Krajinas – Serb-held enclaves in Croatia – aka Sectors South, North, East and West (Map courtesy of UNPROFOR)

So, the call from Knin was a welcome surprise and presented a superb opportunity to spend more time with Sara, from the Canadian Red Cross, of whom I was becoming fonder each time we met. Unless she came across the front lines to Split or I travelled into the Serb-controlled area around Knin, we had no time to get to know each other a bit more.

August 2nd

After passing through the UN, Croatian and ARSK checkpoints on the front line, near the small village of Pakovo Selo, we routinely radioed into the Knin sub-delegation and relayed where we were and our next contact point. My Land Cruiser number was 377,

Destroyed tank at Pakovo Selo ARSK checkpoint, 1995

and the radio check was something like, "ICRC Knin, Knin. This is mobile 377, mobile 377, do you copy, over?" Then providing Knin heard, they would respond with, "Mobile 377, 377. This is ICRC Knin. Please go ahead." I would then say, "Passing Pakovo Selo, next contact Knin." If Knin couldn't hear or respond, Split, Zagreb or any other delegation who heard the call would take up the radio traffic and confirm my message, then relay it back to Knin on their much more powerful land-based radio sets. This system ensured that any

ICRC delegation could track our whereabouts from start to finish of the field trip. Then a few kilometres before the destination, "ICRC Knin, Knin. This is mobile 377, mobile 377, just entering Knin. Will be in delegation in fifteen minutes." Knin would respond with, "OK, Roger. Well copied. See you soon." For security reasons, using names over the radio was frowned upon as all parties monitored the airwaves, but I welcomed the friendly voice.

Negotiating frontline crossings and checkpoints, no matter how often I did, was stressful. At the entrance to the town, there was an ARSK checkpoint – sometimes manned, sometimes not. I always stopped, got out, walked over and said hello to the bored soldier, shared small talk about the war, the weather and football. He would hand over a grubby glass half-full of Rakia and after gulping it down, I would be on my way.

Emma was the new ICRC Knin Head of Sub-Delegation, Swiss-German, and very evidently in charge. The former head had been an American-Swiss guy, who I'd thought was cool and laid back; he smoked cigars too. Soon after Sara arrived to take over from the former medical delegate, she assessed that he was burnt out and needed to be given a complete rest. He had been holed up in his apartment for several weeks, not coming into the delegation. Further, he and the former medical delegate had stopped speaking to each other. After Sara's report and persistence, he was relieved of his position and flown back to the States.

The sub-delegation had an expat staff of three – Emma, Sara and Claire, who was Swiss-French and our general delegate. Claire, the youngest of the three women, had great energy, a terrific sense of humour and sported an array of trendy spectacles. Her duties were to support Emma in her work, hold regular discussions with interlocutors, including the local authorities, perform tracing activities and visit the local jails and prisons to ensure that the Geneva Conventions were being adhered to. Emma's job was to run the operation – no small feat.

Emma asked me into her office and explained the situation in South Krajina, especially in the capital Knin. Her key information included when we could expect an attack and where the Croatian Army were likely to penetrate. Emma was deployed to Knin from her position with the ICRC during the civil war in Sri Lanka. In civilian life, she was a lawyer, as many of the heads of delegation were. As I listened to her, I was impressed with her grasp of the situation.

The Knin Fortress, the second-largest fortress in Croatia, had been a significant defensive stronghold built of limestone in the tenth century, and remained a historic symbol. It sits high above the town. During hot summer months, it was a place to relax in a cool breeze; it boasted an excellent restaurant, which often had fresh fish on the menu, a delicacy in the enclave. Sara and Emma frequently had dinner there; sitting outside, they listened to the artillery fire coming from Dinara, the mountain they could almost touch, the other side of which was Bosnia.

After the briefing and a cup of tea, I drove over to the warehouse with Sara's field officer. She was a welcome change from my field officers in Split. Those young guys knew the job, but after travelling for three to four sixteen-hour days in a Land Cruiser with them, it was nice to have different company.

Many of the villages in the Krajinas that bordered on Croatia had no running water. The reservoirs and infrastructure had been destroyed at the start of the war, and any remaining flow from Croatia had been cut off. Part of the work Emma wanted me to perform was to continue to deliver potable water to the villages, where we had installed large water bladders. So, after picking up the Volvo twelve-tonne water tanker, having a capacity of 4,000 litres, and filling it from Knin's fire station, we drove to the small town of Drniš, about thirty kilometres outside of Knin. There, we filled the empty water bladders for the population's use. We had six in this one town alone and before I arrived, the local driver delivered water there once a week. There were dozens of towns in the same situation, and I expected to be busy just delivering water. On the way back to Knin after the standard radio check-in, we refilled the water tanker. No one knew what would happen over the next days, and the full tanker proved to be very useful indeed.

Volvo twelve-tonne water tanker – Knin, South Krajina, 1995

That evening Sara and Claire invited me to their residence for dinner and to stay. They shared a three-bedroom middle floor of a house, and visiting delegates often used the third bedroom. The owners occupied the upper floor, and their parents occupied the ground floor. The delegates routinely worked long six-day weeks, so most ICRC residences employed a local woman as a housekeeper, who would do the laundry and sometimes leave a cooked dinner. This arrangement helped the fatigued delegates and also provided some local employment.

The town still had power and water, so after unpacking and taking a decent shower, we had dinner and then sat with a welcome glass of wine and chatted until midnight, blissfully unaware of what was soon to happen.

August 3rd

The beautiful morning promised a hot day. The delegation started work at eight, and Sara had been there since seven. Claire was another matter. I was in the kitchen having a coffee when in she burst with her transistor radio, turned up full volume. She had over-slept as usual and was running around the kitchen, trying to get dressed, make coffee, do her hair and a dozen other things, generally achieving none of them. She was always late for work, but no one minded as she did more than her fair share, was excellent at her job and often worked on late into the evening.

The delegation was a four-minute walk from our house. Claire had just run out the door, and I soon followed. There was a hive of activity with everyone busy at their desks, including Emma and three local staff, our field officers. We also had our Welcome Desk receptionist, Melina, and our radio room experts, Mario and Tamara. At the warehouse, we had another two local staff.

I headed out in the German MAN sixteen-tonne tail-lift-equipped truck, taking six local daily workers to a sand quarry just beyond the town. Our job was to fill as many sandbags as we needed to finish off our bomb shelter, started weeks previously. "Bomb shelter" was rather a grand term, really it was just a full-height basement, two-thirds below ground, with four small windows and a garage door. Sandbags were needed to protect the one-third above-ground section.

I had another local driver with me to train on driving the truck, until he was taken away to the army, like the first driver. All large trucks have many gears, and this one was no exception. It was a six-over-six with the top four speeds able to be split. The range change button and the splitter are the same, giving sixteen speeds in total.

I had my student's full attention as I went through the gears on the way to the quarry.

"Start off in four low; no need to use the lowest three gears, as they are only necessary on very steep gradients."

"Five low, six low, not forgetting to double-clutch with each gear change."

"Range change button up into high range, no need to double-clutch from low to high."

"Back to first gear but in high range then second high, now we can use the splitter, three high split down, three high split up, four high split down, four high split up, and so on, until you have reached your desired velocity or your destination."

By this time, he looked like he was going to burst into tears. I was not displeased, as the longer it took him to master the gearbox, the longer I could stay in Knin. And the more time I could spend with Sara.

All morning, we loaded forty-pound sandbags. Just before I decided to return to the delegation around noon, a large-calibre shell, probably a 140-millimetre howitzer, exploded on the rocky hillside 500 metres away. The local workers didn't seem to be worried at all. I had been to Knin many times in the previous sixteen months and had never heard any artillery fire there before. Judging from the direction the shell was fired, Emma's information on the possible area of attack seemed accurate. The Croatian Army was closing in.

Back at the delegation, we started stacking the sandbags, trying to get the bomb shelter finished. The process approximated laying bricks, with each new bag placed halfway across the lower one to make a strong bond. After a couple of hours in the sun, I bought the guys a bottle of beer; we sat down for a moment to cool off and catch our breath. After the second bottle, I decided to call it a day. Only the sandbagging of the front remained unfinished.

Emma was not happy about the unfinished job. Over the previous two weeks, she had been stocking emergency supplies, everything we would need in the event of a large-scale attack. She was convinced something big was brewing. The radio room was set up in the bunker. We had 2,600 litres of drinking water, 1,200 litres of diesel, a large Honda generator, tools, lots of medical equipment, rations, mattresses, blankets and heaps of other emergency equipment.

Twelve months previously, while working out of Zagreb, I had met Tommy, a Canadian truck driver who soon returned to Nova Scotia. Imagine my surprise when I heard a familiar voice calling to me. Tommy had signed on for another mission. He had just brought one truck full of supplies from the warehouse in Zagreb and was going to head back there in the morning. He was staying in the transit residence, so that evening, we invited him for a meal at our place. Sara, Claire, Tommy and I chatted until late; sometimes, the distant rumble of the shelling on Dinara could be clearly heard. It was such a beautiful night, though, and the war seemed so far away.

August 4th

I woke at 2 a.m. to the sound of outgoing artillery fire; not many rounds, only three or four. I thought that unusual but went back to sleep. I had more important stuff to worry about, like how Sara and I could sneak off for a weekend away in the Plitviče Lakes National Park, a world heritage site in Sector North. Since the war started, the tourists had vanished. We had recently made a day trip there on a Sunday with Claire, a visiting delegate from the BRC, and our landlord's fifteen-year-old son, Zlatko. We had a great day and could barely get Zlatko out of the water; his day of swimming was the gift of a temporary escape.

Two hours later, Claire woke us up saying she just had a call from her acquaintance in the UN camp, on the other side of town, warning us to get to our shelter as soon as possible. They were expecting a large-scale attack at 5 a.m. I phoned Tommy at the transit residence and told him to get to the delegation – as soon as possible! Claire had informed Emma, who was in her apartment close to the delegation. I put the kettle on for a brew. My two housemates were rushing around sorting out what to take with them. Not me, though, the seasoned humanitarian worker.

"Don't panic. We'll be back in bed before seven."

They both gave me a sideways look and continued packing. Thinking we had better alert others, I ran upstairs and knocked; after what seemed ages, Stanko, the owner of the house, answered. I explained what we thought was going to happen very shortly.

"I'll do what I can to protect my family," he said.

Stanko was a Bosnian soldier, and he did at least own a vehicle, old and worn out, but a vehicle, nonetheless. Back downstairs, Sara and Claire were gulping down their tea. Honestly, I believed this was a false alarm, but I had to admit there was a definite feeling of tension in the air.

I didn't collect clothes or anything useful, of course, but I did remember to carry my bicycle down. Later, I regretted not having socks or boots. In the half-light, we met Tommy on the way, and as we hurried along, I thought, *There is no way they'll attack on such a beautiful morning as this.*

At the delegation, Emma was already down in the shelter with the radios and other communication gear turned on. Our night guard, Tommy and I went outside to finish off the sandbagging. The section that needed to be done was four metres long and half a metre high. Even at this early hour, the weather was warm, promising another hot day. Tommy and I worked fast to get the job done, until two minutes past five. Emma had told us to be back inside at five. Our guard thought this was a huge joke and was not helping a whole lot. We didn't see the joke. We managed to get most of the section built, though not as well as I would have liked. As we were finishing, the three women were frantically carrying all the office equipment down into the shelter. Emma knew that looters would follow the frontline troops.

Informing our landlord of the coming Storm – Knin, 1995

"Ha!" I said to Tommy, "If they're going to start the attack at five, then they're late."

Just as I finished speaking, *Whoosh BOOM, whoosh BOOM, whoosh BOOM!* The opening salvos of Operation Storm landed almost on top of us.

I've never moved so fast in my life; I bolted into the delegation, not forgetting to slam the door behind me. I did forget Tommy and our guard outside. They followed me down into the shelter just as another salvo of high-explosive artillery shells came screaming down, blowing in all our windows. Tommy, our guard and I ended up in a heap at the bottom of the stairs. We sorted ourselves out and quickly moved into the safest section of the shelter, the radio room, where I stacked some mattresses up against one wall. Our guard then left to try to get his family to safety. Tommy and I huddled with the three women on the floor. The bombardment was becoming much heavier as the Croatian artillerymen, some five kilometres away, warmed to their task.

The glass on top of the garage door cracked with the explosions. Tommy and I Scotch Taped over it, hoping to stop the glass from flying inside. The radio room had one large beam of heavy wood across the ceiling supported by two equally heavy pieces of wood on each side, however they were not nailed or fixed securely. Every explosion shook the building. I watched the posts and beams closely. As soon as I could, I nailed them together. Later, we discovered much of the shelling was with 100- and 155-millimetre shells; a direct hit on the delegation would have penetrated the two floors, right into the shelter.

The delegation was originally a home and was rented out to the ICRC. It was central and had enough parking on-site for vehicles, as no vehicles were left at the residences overnight; thus, our guard. The offices occupied the main floor and a small portion of the second floor, and the basement was converted into the radio room, storage room and now bunker. Most houses in the former Yugoslavia were constructed of hollow, baked clay blocks. A high-velocity AK-47 round fired close enough would penetrate the blocks; a well-placed artillery round would destroy the building and everyone inside.

At six that morning, Melina, who lived in the upstairs apartment with her brother and grandmother, came down into the shelter and asked if we knew what was going to happen. We stated that it looked serious and, judging by the intensity of the bombardment, it seemed like the Croatians would soon invade. We asked if she and her family were all right; she assured us that although they were scared, they wanted to stay upstairs.

The Red Cross is typically protected during armed conflict. It certainly seemed as though the shelling was occurring just outside our door so clearly, we were unprotected. We had been in daily, if not more frequent, communication with the UN Canbat in Knin as part of our ongoing work prior to the attack. Yet we were unofficially notified only one hour before the attack by Claire's Swedish friend working as a civilian with the UN, an information technology guy. When we spoke with him days later, he said he did not ask for permission to inform us and called as soon as he realized what was going to happen. It was clear that the Canbat knew about the coming of Operation Storm but didn't inform us; perhaps because of security concerns – who knows?

In all my time in the former Yugoslavia, I had never experienced anything like the sustained ferocity and duration of this attack. Typically, a few artillery rounds would be fired at random into towns, generally in the evening when lots of young people were promenading on the main street. Sometimes it only took one or two shells in the right place to claim many innocent lives.

Two short months before Oluja, on May 25th at five minutes to nine one lovely summer evening in Tuzla, the ARSK fired one 130-millimetre high-explosive fragmentation shell aimed at the main street, killing seventy-one and injuring 240 young people, all between the ages of eighteen and twenty-five. It was apparent to me that this attack on Knin had a different intention.

Someone was constantly at the radio trying to contact our head of delegation in Zagreb or any other sub-delegations around the country to provide an update on the situation. None of us were trained to operate the satellite communications. Tommy and I were proficient with the VHF sets, but these had limited range, so were no help at all in this circumstance. Understandably, our local staff radio operators were not in for work that morning. When we did manage to raise someone in another delegation, they gave us what information they had and, most importantly, moral support.

The artillery bombardment was constant and frighteningly heavy for fifteen to twenty minutes. Then it either passed over to another part of town or stopped for a few minutes before resuming. During the shelling, four of us sat on a mattress with our backs against the wall while Tommy was sound asleep on the couch.

First radio contact with ICRC Zagreb during Operation Storm, the bunker – 1995

When there was a brief pause, we developed a comforting routine. Claire would visit the toilet, Sara would sweep up, Emma would man the radio, I would boil water for a cup of tea and Tommy would get into a more comfortable sleeping position on the couch. I couldn't figure out how someone could sleep during this terrifying storm of steel. Later, I realized he had only just flown in from the east coast of Canada and had jet lag. We each had our own way of coping with the genuine possibility of the house taking a direct hit and what might happen in the aftermath.

Although we didn't know at the time, the house and roof did sustain some shrapnel and blast damage. Our rooftop radio mast was knocked down and damaged but luckily was still functioning. The closest a shell landed was two metres from the shelter, in gravel on the edge of the road; it buried itself before exploding. If it had been half a metre closer on the concrete path, our hastily erected sandbag shelter would have been severely tested.

My thoughts, all of ours, were with the civilian population beyond our shelter walls.

In the shelter, I struggled to keep my nerves in check, especially when the shelling reached its peak. I had a Red Cross helmet, but my personal flak jacket was still in our apartment. As we sat together on the mattress during the shelling, Tommy shared his jacket with me. When it lay across our chests during the periods of heavy shelling or when one landed particularly close, I found myself surreptitiously pulling the jacket millimetre by millimetre over to my side. Tommy was doing the same. If a shell had penetrated the shelter, our flak jackets would have been as much protection as a clean T-shirt.

During all this, I was imagining what would happen if we had a direct hit and were buried under the house. It would be dark and dusty. There would be panic, disorientation and most likely some injuries. In a quiet moment, I spoke with Tommy to make sure we both knew where the pickaxe, shovel, sledgehammer, crowbar and flashlights were, and that we had some sort of plan to get us all out of the bunker should the house collapse.

Melina shouted down to Sara to come quickly; there was a badly wounded soldier outside on the front step. Sara, Tommy and I ran upstairs to find a Serbian soldier covered in blood, asking for a drink of water. He was in pain and shock. The shells were raining down heavily again, so we quickly brought him inside and shut the door. Melina supported him on one side and I on the other.

"Has he got a weapon?" Sara asked.

He had, so I unbuckled his belt; as much as he could, he helped me remove his pistol. Armies across the world knew and mostly respected the no weapons rule – except, of course, when the situation for the warring parties became desperate. Then our rules, the rules of war or anyone else's rules meant nothing, as we were soon to discover.

We helped the soldier into the shelter, where we laid him on a mattress at the bottom of the stairs. The shelling remained heavy and deafening. He was losing a lot of blood that was beginning to soak through the mattress. Sara took charge of the situation and gave Tommy, Melina and me instructions on how to stop the bleeding. We cut off his blood-soaked combat trousers, and each of us knelt alongside him in ten-minute relays, applying field dressings and pressure on the wounds. Our hands were covered in his blood; I could see Sara was checking him for any other injuries. Forty minutes later, just as we were managing to slow down his blood loss, the power went out. It was broad daylight outside but not in the shelter.

We were plunged into darkness. Since the mouldy bread and cheese incident, I carried a small mag light torch on a key ring in my pocket. I held it in my mouth and kept trying to stop this soldier from bleeding to death. Sara started the emergency generator. How she knew the procedure, I didn't know, but start it she did. Twenty-five minutes later, we managed to stabilize him. He was one lucky soldier; had he not been hit outside our delegation, he would have bled to death.

He had numerous shrapnel and puncture wounds around his stomach and groin, glass in one eye and a broken ankle. Sara didn't have any medical tape handy, so we used a roll of duct tape and wrapped his wounds with that. His name was Josip, and he was extremely hirsute; he must have suffered absolute agony when the tape was eventually removed.

We were now relying solely on our generator to power the lights and the radio. It was in a small room at the bottom of the stairs, along with the fuel, tools, spare parts and around two-thirds of our emergency water supply. Tommy or I refuelled the machine every four hours. The exhaust was running out through a small window, but the heat from the engine was incredible, up to forty-six degrees centigrade. After the quarter-hour it took to fill it with fuel, we were nearly overcome by the heat and noise. It was a most unpleasant but essential job. Without a generator, we had no ability to contact anyone on the radio and let them know our circumstances.

When we were working on Josip, Emma contacted the Zagreb delegation and asked if there was any way to notify the military authorities. We in Knin had no way to speak with or contact any of the warring parties during the shelling. When we needed to contact any of the armed forces in the area, a delegate would phone and arrange an in-person meeting. Zagreb did have a line of communication open with the ARSK and arranged to have our soldier collected and taken to the Knin hospital.

At close to 8:30 a.m., we heard pounding on the door: two soldiers to pick up their wounded colleague. We helped carry Josip upstairs and put him in the ambulance. I was expecting a proper military vehicle with red crosses and blue lights flashing. Instead, we loaded this fellow onto the floor of a small family van. The soldiers told us they had been cruising the town, collecting the dead and wounded since 5 a.m., in the midst of non-stop shelling, wearing only T-shirts and combat fatigues. Two very brave men. The few minutes we were outside were terrifying due to the unpredictability of the shelling. In contrast to the roar of the bombardment and Josip's serious injuries, the weather was serene; shining sun on a beautiful summer morning. Nobody was around, aside from the occasional vehicle containing civilians or soldiers, roaring past at breakneck speed.

Later, during a pause in the shelling, I went outside to see what might have caused Josip's injuries. His car, a small Yugoslav-built Lada, had been hit directly on the engine block in front of the driver. Depending on the trajectory of the shell, the blast and shrapnel generally follow the direction of flight. Because the round was fired from behind, almost all the shrapnel was directed away from him. He was lucky to be alive.

Broken glass glinted everywhere. I inhaled the acrid stench of vehicle tires and burning buildings, and heard the *crump*, *crump*, and *whoosh*

BOOM! Any shells landing close by reverberated like rolling thunder in a heavy storm. When I was outside, I collected a couple of spare helmets and flak jackets from one of our Land Cruisers. Each Cruiser should have had full equipment in the back; luckily, this one did. Now I had my own jacket, I decided to wear it all the time. After a quick look around, I hustled back into the shelter.

Our three delegation Land Cruisers were parked around the back, mostly out of sight from the road. If we got a chance, I thought Tommy and I should remove at least one wheel on each and hide it. When the Croatian troops did finally enter the town, they would want the vehicles. As it turned out, I should have done this when I first thought about it.

Tommy and I carried the blood-soaked mattress upstairs, ready to be put out when the shelling eased off. We also secured the floor supports with more nails. Emma and Claire were talking with Zagreb. Just then, Melina came into the radio room to say there was a soldier upstairs demanding a Land Cruiser.

Despite continued heavy shelling, Emma and I went upstairs to see what was going on. The young, fully armed and very frightened Serbian soldier, who only wanted to get away from the inferno, was in the middle of a rather heated discussion with Melina. She faced him down, explaining that we were the Red Cross, not the UN, which he probably already knew, and that we had just saved the life of one of his colleagues.

"Is this true?" he said.

"Of course, it's true!" Melina shouted, by this time quite cross, as we wanted to get back down to the relative safety of the shelter. Hearing this, he calmed down a little. Then, to my surprise, he reached out, shook my hand and ran out the front door. We never saw him again, but later we had visitors we were not able to calm down quite so easily. If the attack continued, I knew this was just the start of people wanting our vehicles.

About this time, Emma had the four of us alone in the radio room. She looked at each of us and asked, "Would you like to leave and go to the UN camp, or would you like to stay here?" We didn't hesitate and answered in unison that we would stay at the delegation; it was where we felt we were needed.

The shelling was easing off; ten minutes later, Mario appeared in the radio room and started improving our communications set-up. As the roof aerial had been damaged, he could not do much to fix the reception. None of us thought it a good idea to get on the roof to sort it out. Fifteen minutes later, just as the shelling was growing in intensity again, Tamara, our other radio operator, strolled in, looking calm and composed. Tamara was six months pregnant with her first child. Our local staff coming into work demonstrated the humanitarian dedication of all Red Cross personnel. Mario and Tamara showed extraordinary bravery and selflessness. Both staff had family in town that they were obviously concerned about. Mario was an example of the general Yugoslavian population. He was a Croatian, living in a Serb-held enclave, with his Serbian wife.

It was a relief to have them at the radio doing what they were trained to do. It supported Emma, Sara and Claire to do the hundred other things demanding their attention. It was now 9 a.m. and after four hours of mostly continuous shelling, we were all tired and stressed. The worst part was not knowing where the next shell would land or when the shelling would stop. It eventually did – *thirty-two hours later.*

Around noon, the mayor of Knin and one local man came down into the shelter and demanded we evacuate as many women and children as possible to the countryside, where it was thought to be safer. Everyone presumed only Knin was under attack. No one knew at that time that the whole of the Krajina was threatened.

Emma explained to the mayor that it was too dangerous to be outside, "And no, we cannot do this." If humanitarian workers put themselves in harm's way and became casualties, what good were they? So, unless there was no choice, we would wait until at least the active fighting slowed down before venturing outside the shelter.

"So be it, we'll return with weapons and take the vehicles," the townsmen said.

Hmmm, this doesn't sound good. In extreme circumstances, people will do what they need to survive. This put us, and especially Emma, as our leader, in a tricky position. It seemed like we had two choices: to risk our lives and try to save a truckload of women and children and maybe our vehicles or take no risk and lose our vehicles. If we employed the second option, when we could go outside and get to work, we would have no vehicles to work with. The first option was no small feat either, evacuating a truckload of civilians. But back to option two: we also knew there were many people who would need help and assistance when the fighting eventually stopped.

I managed to take Emma aside to suggest that I would go to our warehouse and get the MAN truck. It had a tail lift and could take one load of women and children out of the town to safety. She was absolutely against it at first, but eventually agreed it was the best choice in a bad situation. I wasn't being particularly brave, but I was getting increasingly nervous as the shelling continued. I felt I had to get out of the shelter and do something, never mind the danger. As the mayor was leaving, we told him our plan.

We spoke to Melina and Mario; to their eternal credit, they agreed to come with me. Emma wanted me to take Melina as a translator and for Mario to take a Land Cruiser in case the MAN broke down. I was very happy to have them both along. After donning helmets and flak jackets, we jumped into the Land Cruiser and drove as fast as was safe through the town while trying to avoid broken glass, smashed roof tiles and furniture blown out of shell-blasted buildings. It was a nightmare trip to our warehouse, four kilometres away. We passed many burning buildings, civilian and military vehicles caught by shells, and smoking shell holes in the road. Everywhere, people were fleeing for their lives, Serb soldiers in their military vehicles, and a few civilians in cars and trucks. Those on old farm tractors were often pulling equally old trailers, loaded down with the few possessions that families could grab in panic. Some rode bicycles; others trundled wheelbarrows holding an infirm relative. *How far can you push a person sitting in a wheelbarrow?* Some were just simply running away from the murderous attack on the town. I clearly remember negotiating around a large ARSK troop carrier on its side after being hit by a shell with a fire just beginning to take hold. I don't know what happened to those soldiers; I didn't dare look too closely.

After what seemed eons but was closer to fifteen minutes, we got to the warehouse. This too had taken a direct hit. A shell had exploded on impact with the roof, making a nine by five metre hole. The blast and shrapnel had destroyed much of our supplies of food parcels and blankets. Sara's small medical storage part of the warehouse seemed undamaged; her Land Cruiser had a smashed windscreen but was usable. Outside, where the other vehicles were parked, the three trucks had suffered greater damage. My favourite, the old Volvo water tanker, had also been blasted by shrapnel. It looked like the water tank itself was OK, but there were many holes elsewhere. It was a beautiful-looking truck and a shame to see it damaged. The newer Scania that Tommy had brought down from Zagreb looked OK, but my focus was on the MAN. Both side windows were blown out, and the driver's door hung open, as the lock had been blasted off. But the fuel tank and tires looked OK.

I told Melina to sit at the back of the driver's seat and hold the door shut. Mario was to proceed in the Land Cruiser, not mess around, drive fast and stay out of my way. The MAN had a powerful 300-horsepower motor and was almost as fast as the underpowered Land Cruiser. The shelling was not letting up, so we moved quickly.

As frightening as it was being outside, I was happy to be doing something rather than waiting helplessly in the bunker. Mario and

Melina may have thought otherwise. Mario drove off after we got the truck started and headed back into town. I was boxed in by the Scania, the Volvo and a security fence. Without any hesitation, with Melina clinging to my door, I drove right through the security fence with, luckily, no punctures. Our trip back to the centre of the town was as harrowing as the trip to the warehouse had been.

The large army truck was by now fully ablaze with the spilled diesel burning across the road. We had to hurtle through and hope for the best. As long as we kept moving, I figured we would not be affected by the flames.

On our way back to the delegation, we saw that mayhem ruled the streets. It seemed a little quieter in our part of town; perhaps most people had already fled or still cowered in their homes. Minutes later, I found they had not all fled. Reversing down to an area between twelve storey blocks, I saw a mob of hysterical people in my rear-view mirror. I really did not want to deal with this, but I had to. Helping Melina down from the cab, we went to the back of the truck to lower the tail lift. People were too close; we couldn't open it enough to start lowering it. Melina and I tried to convince everyone to make room. After a lot of pushing and shouting, I managed to get it lowered halfway to enable people to get on board.

During all this, Mario, who had parked the Land Cruiser along-side the truck, sat white-faced. I shouted to him to come over and help, but he was rooted on the spot, mute with fear, watching the scene in front of him. I was pushed aside as a mob of terrified people tried to scramble on board. The younger ones got on quickly. The older folks and women with two or three small children and bags were struggling to get a place on the rapidly filling truck. After elbowing my way through, I finally managed to jump up onto the tail lift and tried to let on only women and children, as per our discussion with the mayor and his sidekick. It was almost impossible to regulate who got on and who didn't.

One soldier jumped on, and I immediately pushed him off. He got up and pointed his weapon at me to show what would happen if he didn't get on board. Another man also jumped on. Later, I was very glad the two men did get on the truck. I believe their presence saved Melina's life.

The shelling was still heavy and deafening, falling randomly all over the town. Once the truck was packed full of terrified people, I closed the lift and raised it, ready to leave. I could not speak above a whisper due to the car tires ablaze, the burning buildings, the heat and thirst, and the sheer raw tension of the moment. I ran over to Mario who was still staring blankly and shook him.

"Go in front Mario, you know where we're going!"

His Land Cruiser was full, with ten people jammed inside.

Loading took maybe twenty minutes. It would have been complete slaughter if a shell had landed anywhere near the truck. There were probably sixty people packed in the back. With Melina holding the door closed, we followed Mario out of town, away from the roaring, chaotic madness.

Knin is surrounded by hills, so once the Croatians gained control of the countryside, they could bombard the town with ease. It looked like they were closing in quickly. After we climbed the hill out of town, heading towards the small village of Zrmanja, forty kilometres north of Knin, the road levelled out. I started to speed up; Mario kept well ahead of us in his overloaded Land Cruiser. There were lots of new shell craters, some still smoking, on the road and in the fields. This surprised me, as I had thought the main thrust of the attack was coming from the south and southeast, but the Croats were advancing from the west as well. Thankfully, the shellfire was less intense out of town but continued sporadically. The scenes we witnessed on the road that day were those one would expect to see in a war movie, except this was the brutal reality of what war could do to ordinary people.

We passed many broken-down tractors, their trailers half-full of belongings, mattresses, blankets, clothing, discarded shoes and children's toys. The columns of terrified people on the road north out of Knin were totally unaware they were not moving away from the attacking Croatian Army but moving parallel to the fighting. The few remaining people in their homes or farms and hamlets had no idea where this storm was coming from or how and when it would end.

Civilians' belongings lost while escaping Knin during Oluja, 1995 – note washboard tank track markings on road

Explosions, noise and fear were their reality. We passed a column of people and vehicles about fifteen kilometres long. Some small children were led by the hand by their older siblings. So many people who, not many hours ago, were thinking about their work, school, farming, and all the normal day-to-day realities. On the road that day, I saw thousands of people, with a few groups of ARSK soldiers among them, trudging northwards to presumed *safety*. Within the next two days, an area of

10,400-square kilometres changed hands. The reports after this exodus estimated that 200,000 people in the Krajina were on the move, the largest mass movement of refugees since the Second World War.

In 2001, the Croatian generals in command were indicted for war crimes during this operation, but later acquitted. There were a couple of genuine Serbian military targets in the town that could have and should have been the only target of the shellfire. Instead, the Croatian military authorities decided to target the civilian population with terror bombing, driving out all the people, the vast majority of whom were women and children. In this respect, they were successful. The Geneva Conventions state that it is a war crime to target non-combatant and civilian areas. This was ethnic cleansing at its most aggressive.

Mario remained in the lead with Melina and I following in the truck with my human cargo. Passing frightened people, we saw some throw rocks at us. The soldiers amongst them, shaking their fists in the air, looked like they would start shooting as we passed. They must have thought, *Even the Red Cross are running away to safety. What use are they when things really turn bad?* I did wonder what they thought when, two hours later, they saw the same two Red Cross vehicles heading back, into the inferno that was Knin.

Ninety minutes later, we turned off the main road to the hamlet of Zrmanja, a run-down and deserted farming community. At the small village square, we stopped. Before getting out, I radioed to the delegation, "Knin, Knin. This is truck 378, truck 378 with Cruiser 483, Cruiser 483, just arrived in Zrmanja. Will contact when leaving, over." Emma, back in the radio room, answered immediately, "Truck 378, truck 378, this is Knin. Received and understood. Standing by, over." Often a quick "copy that – over", was simply two clicks on the mic send button, which is what I did. By the time I had climbed out of the truck, Mario had regained his voice and was talking to Melina. When I started to lower the tail lift, Melina said, "Mario noticed the mayor of Knin was in the back of the truck with his family."

When I opened the rear doors, a wall of heat and the smell of humanity took my breath away. These people were only inside for ninety minutes, but with the August sun and lack of air, I wondered how much longer they would have lasted. As they started to climb down, the soldier I had pushed off the truck back in Knin handed me his AK-47 assault rifle, jumped down with the other man, and held out his hand for his weapon. The old people, women and children also climbed down with the help of others. When everyone was down and stretching their legs, with the children crying and screaming, I could see they were wondering, *What's next?*

The shelling was a distant rumble, but there was clearly no help in the deserted village. I had a bale of blankets in the truck; lowering it to the ground I rolled it up against a wall in the square in case anyone needed one for shelter during the trek through the forests, across the border into Serbia and a displaced persons camp.

"Point out the mayor to me," I said to Melina. "We're taking that bastard back to Knin."

She did. Mario, who was standing nearby, suggested it would be best if I didn't.

Melina and I walked over to the mayor, and I asked her to translate word for word what I said. I decided to confront him for sneaking aboard my truck when I had agreed to take only women and children. I told him that he was a little shit and a coward. Hearing this, he started shouting at us. Melina, by this time in tears, was so angry with him for using his position to get out of Knin that she started calling him things one should not call anyone, especially an angry Serbian male.

As the row escalated, the other man and the soldier came over. Suddenly, the mayor put his hand into his pocket and started to pull out a pistol. I honestly thought he was going to shoot Melina. The two men grabbed the mayor and took him aside. I glanced at the soldier, nodded my thanks and pushed a sobbing Melina up into the cab of my truck. We turned around, Mario in the lead again, and left Zrmanja just as fast as we could. I often wonder what happened to those people we left in that square in the middle of the countryside in the August heat.

Back on the main road, I again radioed in to let Emma know we were returning. This must have eased her worry. With an empty truck, we were able to move faster. Passing by the thousands of desperate people and soldiers going the other way, we received no shouted abuse, stones or threats.

I was sure that Mario and Melina, who both had family in Knin, were dreading re-entering the town where many buildings were ablaze. It was now after 4 p.m.; upon arriving at the top of the hill before entering Knin, I radioed Mario to go on to the warehouse and told him I'd be there in five minutes. I looked out across the town and saw a scene of devastation; the flow of people was much less, but more buildings had been hit, windows blown out, with flames taking hold and burning fiercely. Much more smoke shrouded the town. The shelling had been almost nonstop since five that morning, and eleven hours later showed no sign of stopping.

Our residence was on the way into town, so I asked Melina to stay in the truck while I ran in to get a change of clothes. She seemed happy to take a break from kneeling at the rear of my seat, holding the door closed. I ran upstairs and grabbed my bag containing a box of cigars and a pair of jeans, forgetting to get my other bag containing all the receipts and remaining cash to be eventually returned to the BRC. It was risky leaving the truck parked even for five minutes, and anyone with a weapon would have taken it at gunpoint. The Croatian Army would soon loot anything of any value left in the house. Back in the truck, we headed to the warehouse to meet Mario in an apparent lull in the shelling. I quickly reversed the truck into the warehouse and locked the door. Mario was waiting for us with the engine running, and we drove back to the delegation without any mishaps. We had been outside for almost four hours, running on pure adrenaline, expecting to be shelled or shot at any moment. During those hours, I was totally switched on, at maximum efficiency.

Only when we all got back inside did I realize what a strain on my nerves this business was. I was soaked with sweat but felt quite calm. Sara looked right at me and said, "Are you OK?" Not knowing what else to say, I said, "Yes." She then went and comforted Melina, who was very upset over the mayor affair. I sat down with Tommy and drank a large glass of Rakia, normally sipped from a small shot glass. I think I was still running on one hundred percent adrenaline, as the plum brandy had no effect on me at all.

Mario and Melina left soon and went home to arrange for their families' departure. Tommy and I warmed up something for the five of us remaining in the radio room to eat. We had a one-ring burner to cook on and British Army ration packs. It was 8 p.m., and the shelling continued. Fifteen hours thus far. We had been so tense and busy that no one was at all hungry, but we ate anyway.

The Croatian Army, judging by the intensity of the shelling, must have decided to enter the town the next day. They wouldn't move during darkness because it was safer in the daylight. We discovered much later that they had 130,000 troops; seventeen Soviet-built MiG fighter bombers, eleven of which sustained damage from AA ground fire; and, for Knin alone, thirty Soviet T-55 main battle tanks. The name of the operation, *Storm*, was well chosen.

It was dark outside; burning buildings supplied the only illumination in the town. Melina's sixteen-year-old brother had a small Lada parked outside the delegation. He had kept his little car in working order but rarely drove it due to the four-year embargo on fuel. His car was going to be his family's means of escape, but unfortunately a piece of shrapnel had punctured the fuel tank. He lost the few precious litres of gas he had been saving. The shelling had eased off again, but not completely, still terrifying in its randomness. We could hear small arms firing on the outskirts of the town. Melina's brother was scared, and angry as well because of the hole in his fuel tank. He had rigged up a one-litre plastic Coca-Cola bottle under the bonnet with a plastic pipe running to the carburettor. "The pipe is not long enough," he said desperately. I felt bad for the young man, and in any other circumstance, I would have helped him, but at that moment, I had so many other things to do. He then ran upstairs, and ten minutes later, I saw him trying to rig another pipe to the carb. He now had an AK-47 assault rifle slung over his back. If the unwelcome visitors to the town saw him with this weapon slung across his back, he would be shot. No questions asked, simply shot.

Mario, Melina, Tamara and their families were now crowded into the bunker, twelve people in all. They were going to head north and try to reach Serbia and safety. I wondered, *In what?* The situation in the airless shelter was extremely tense, with everyone frightened and shouting. I explained to Emma, who was trying to sort out a dozen things, that none of the local staff had any reliable means of transport. Even if they could find a farm tractor, it was too late, and they would get caught up in the fighting before they got very far. Several of the men were of military age, thus at risk.

She barely looked up from the communications equipment. "Okay, give them a Cruiser." Tommy and I herded everybody upstairs and told Mario to get everyone into the vehicle we chose. Ten adults packed themselves into the Cruiser, while two small children waited to get onto their mothers' laps. Tommy and I had helmets and flak jackets on, and to these children, we must have looked menacing. Tommy caught one and put her in the back with her mother. I had difficulty catching the other boy but eventually handed him, wriggling and screaming, to his mum. I slammed the door shut and ran around the front to tell Mario to move fast. Had anyone seen a vehicle parked with the lights on, that would also have been taken at gunpoint.

"There's not enough fuel," Mario yelled. I went to the back of the Cruiser, opened the door again and pushed in a 25-litre jerrycan of diesel and wished them good luck. Off they drove into the darkness, punctuated by shellfire flashes.

It was a relief to see them go but also very sad. We had worked closely together. They were more than just local staff; they were friends.

Much later, when the situation had settled down, we heard from ICRC Belgrade that they had arrived safely and handed in the Land Cruiser. We were immensely relieved and cheered out loud!

The departure took about twenty minutes. I had one last look around; down the dark street, I glimpsed a few people moving cautiously in the shadows between the deserted buildings. I heard shouting, saw the glow of the fires, inhaled the acrid taste of smoke, then followed Tommy inside just as the shelling intensified again. It was 11 p.m., and we were back to the five of us.

I believed the situation would soon become even more unstable as the last few desperate people tried to leave town. Our building was the only one in town that had any electric power. We had all the lights on as a beacon for anyone who needed help or shelter. When the Croats did arrive, we wanted our building recognized as a Red Cross establishment and spared any destruction. Given what had been done and what was still occurring under the banner of ethnic cleansing in the whole of the former Yugoslavia over the past four years, I was not feeling too confident about what the next hours might bring.

Two old ladies and one old man, all dressed in their Sunday best, too frail to escape, joined us in the shelter. They sat on hard chairs outside the radio room, shocked silent. Because of the constantly running generator, the noise and heat were almost unbearable. We had no choice; to go upstairs to the office would be too risky as we could hear heavy machine gunfire, as well as small-arms fire all over town. Emma asked me to estimate how much generator fuel we had left. We had 1,000 litres in jerrycans, so we were good for three weeks if the generator ran constantly. One thing did concern me; each time we filled up, we checked the oil level and had to top it up. We only had one three-gallon can in total, but I was pretty sure the fighting would cease before we ran out of oil. We'd see.

When we left our residence at four-thirty that morning, I wore a T-shirt, rolled up jeans and sandals (no socks, as that's not cool); we all knew it would be another hot day in Knin. There was not one window-pane of glass left in the whole town, and the ground was covered by a blanket of shards. During my exploits outside over the course of the day, my feet became a mass of tiny cuts and quite sore.

The excitement had been going on for eighteen and a half hours. Both radios were in constant use, with one or two of the women replying to the incessant questions from ICRC Zagreb or headquarters in Geneva. They were magnificent to watch, coping with the unrelenting radio traffic.

I looked around and noticed Sara was not in the shelter. I asked Tommy if he knew where she was.

"Upstairs talking to a soldier."

I went up and saw her standing at the front door talking to a combat ready ARSK soldier. He was one of the doctors Sara knew well from her work with him in an outlying area of South Krajina. He did not look like he was there to treat anyone. Sara and I talked with him for fifteen minutes, standing just inside the front door, hoping the shells still falling over the town would land elsewhere. He wanted a Cruiser to take his family to safety. We explained why he couldn't take a Cruiser, which of course he already knew. After he left, we locked the front door. We were sure he would return.

"Shh!" said Claire, two hours later. "I hear shooting upstairs."

Twenty seconds later, our doctor came bursting into the radio room, sweating in terror. He knew, as we all did, that the Croatian Army would soon be in the town, going from house to house looking for Serbian military or any Serbian male to exact their revenge. We sat on the floor in our usual places against the wall. The shells were still landing all over the town. He was waving his Kalashnikov, ranting and raving, blaming the Red Cross and the international community for the situation. He had just machine-gunned the front door lock off and was in such a frightened state he could have easily murdered us, taken a vehicle and no one would have known.

"Do you want a Cruiser?" I asked.

"Yes!" he screamed.

I grabbed a set of keys and followed him upstairs. Climbing over what was left of the front door, I gave him the keys and told him to go. The two remaining Cruisers were hidden around the back of the delegation and difficult to reverse out onto the road. When he saw how they were parked, he ran back and told me to do it. It was pitch-dark outside; with the shells and shrapnel flying around, I was reluctant to go out. He pointed the muzzle of his rifle at me and although he spoke English well, he didn't need to. I quickly understood what he would do if I didn't comply. I brought the Cruiser alongside the building, jumped out and said, "Now go!"

"No, I cannot reverse it out onto the road," he said.

I did as he wanted and parked it on the road, facing the direction he wanted to go. Then remembering I had a can of white paint ready just inside the front door, I said, "Please wait two minutes and let me paint out the emblems."

This was becoming bizarre, outside amidst the shelling, with a frightened man in the driver's seat with the engine running, I painted the side, bonnet and roof. After thirty seconds, he shouted, "That's enough." As I jumped off the Cruiser, he roared off into the darkness. I'd pushed my luck asking him to wait, but I didn't like the thought of an armed soldier driving around in a fully emblemized Red Cross vehicle. Back downstairs, it was almost cosy, but soon began to feel hot, noisy and stuffy.

Two days later, our doctor dropped off the Land Cruiser at an ICRC delegation in Bosnia, with thanks to us for *lending* it to him.

The vehicle was in good condition. We knew how terrified he was for his family, and we were glad he made it to safety.

Just before Mario left, he gave Sara instructions on how to fax a message through the PACTOR satellite communications system. We knew that ICRC Zagreb and the main office in Geneva were aware of what was happening, and we presumed that ICRC Geneva had contacted our respective National Societies and informed our next of kin of the situation. But as the attack was being broadcast over main news channels around the world, Sara sent faxes to the contacts we gave her. I sent one to a close friend and asked him to phone home and let my parents know we were still in one piece.

August 5th, Day 2

It was 1:30 a.m., and the shelling continued, sometimes close, and other times farther away, but there all the same. The heat and constant static and noise from the radios were getting on my nerves. I think the others must have felt the same. We were all so tired, but there was no chance of sleeping. We knew things would get more dangerous. Each of us supported one another; we realized we needed to make an extra effort in being understanding. Following the action of the previous day, we were a solid team. Each person's tasks continued through any lull. As before, Sara swept the floors, Claire visited the loo, Emma worked the radio, I made tea and Tommy slept. It was kind of reassuring, really – the routines and our coping mechanisms.

The three old folks were still with us, silent, frightened, hungry and thirsty. We almost had to force them to take a drink of water and a little of the food we rustled up.

Now 2:30 a.m., the bombardment seemed to have eased a little. Suddenly, we heard someone upstairs. Before I could get up and see what they wanted (although I really knew it would be a Cruiser), they came crashing into the radio room. Two young, fully armed ARSK soldiers. One look into the faces of these two men, and I knew there would be no discussion. I handed them a set of keys for the last Cruiser we had on-site.

I started to follow them back upstairs as I wanted to deploy my white paint again. Halfway up the stairs, one of the soldiers stopped, turned around and pointed his assault rifle at my chest. "Fuck off," he spat. I turned around, somewhat shaken and decided a cup of tea was in order. The three women were fully absorbed trying to answer the unremitting radio traffic, so Tommy and I made tea and sat down to try to relax a little.

Emma had just finished talking with Geneva on the HF set when she looked at me and said, "Roger, we have more visitors upstairs." We both went up to the strangely quiet offices where, as most of the windows were blown in, a warm breeze wafted through. The continuing clamour from the shelling outside only added to our growing sense of unease. The lights we had left on as a beacon had been turned off. Peering into the semi-darkness, both Emma and I noticed two soldiers with a dog just leaving. They didn't look back, so we stayed silent and watched them go. We never knew what they were doing or what their intentions may have been, but they seemed at that moment, like guardians. While we were upstairs, I took a quick look at the destroyed door to see if I could somehow jam it back into the hole, but it was impossible to fix.

We had been going full-on for twenty-two hours. Emma suggested we all try to get some sleep while she stayed awake to monitor the radio. We each lay on a small mattress on the floor and were instantly asleep. An hour later, "Knin, Knin, this is Zagreb. Do you copy, over?" Emma had also dozed off. I think we would have slept on if Claire hadn't heard the call and answered Zagreb. The shelling was steady and constant. Again, we sat up against the wall wearing helmets and flak jackets, waiting for the dawn. Things were less spooky in the daylight.

At 5:20 a.m., the shelling again intensified. I wondered what was happening outside, and when we could venture out and start doing the work the Red Cross had engaged us to do. Sara and Claire made a plate of bread and jam with a pot of tea. We sat eating, looking at each other, wondering what the day would bring. We were on edge, not knowing if a high-explosive projectile would crash through the shelter roof and explode amongst us.

After breakfast, I decided to have a wash and shave and change my clothes. I wondered how long we could continue on almost no sleep. Soon I would refill the generator with diesel and would once more be bathed in sweat. It was sheer bliss to be able to change my bloodied jeans for a clean pair.

By 8 a.m., the demonic drumfire shelling had eased off again. The artillerymen must also have needed a break. Sara and I decided to go upstairs to see what was happening outside. Shards of glass glinted everywhere; pieces of paper, ash and other debris blew around. The air reeked of burning tires and burning buildings. We saw no one under the already blazing sun; it was going to be another long, scorching day. We didn't linger. The shelling had been replaced by a lot of small-arms and some heavy-machine-gun fire. I wanted to finish off the sandbagging, but it was just too dangerous. A little later, Tommy and I hung two large Red Cross flags on either side of the building. The delegation was well emblemized, but two more flags flying in the breeze could only help.

Around ten the shelling resumed. We appeared to be reasonably calm and under control, but if the others felt anything like I did, they were thinking, *Please God, make this stop.* We knew the house-to-house fighting would be next. I thought I might welcome that as a reprieve from the bloody shelling. *Still, never mind, nothing any of us could do about it.*

"Let's have a cup of tea."

Since we had been in the shelter, I had probably made fifty cups of tea. It gave me something to do to take my mind off the situation. *Besides, Englishmen are supposed to make tea in times of great danger, aren't they?*

We got most of our information about the scale of Operation Storm through our small television set tuned into the BBC or Sky News. Half the time, the reports were wrong. The BBC reported that the town of Knin had fallen, and there were many bodies lying in the streets. We didn't know how many dead and wounded there were, but judging by the volume of small-arms fire, the fighting was still ferocious, so we knew the town had not fallen just yet. As we were watching Sky News, we saw our wounded soldier sitting in bed in the Knin hospital, smiling at the camera. A courageous skeleton staff of doctors and nurses had stayed behind to care for any new cases and the few patients too old or too ill to move.

Sitting down with the four others huddled against the wall as the bombardment continued, I thought to myself how lucky I was to be in Knin during this time. If the call for an expat driver had come in a day later, or if I had postponed for just one day, and if Tommy had postponed coming from Zagreb also by just one day, then the three women would have been totally alone. I'm not sure what I would have done if I had been held up in Split when Operation Storm was unleashed, knowing Sara, Emma and Claire were alone. I like to think I would have used my Cruiser to drive through the fighting to Knin. Who knows? It was tense enough crossing the front lines when there was no active fighting.

At 1 p.m., we thought the shelling really had stopped, so I went for another look outside. I heard a tremendous amount of small-arms fire all over town, mainly Croatian soldiers simply shooting into houses and apartment buildings. As I stood there, in a rare moment of quiet, a distant rumble turned into an earthshattering roar. Stunned and momentarily deafened, I saw a Croatian MiG-21 at rooftop height with full after-burner on vanish upwards into the clouds. The staggering force was breathtakingly spectacular; no doubt it had its intended victorious effect on the town.

CHAPTER 12

Knin

• • • • •

As I was standing in the delegation doorway, an excited soldier brandishing his AK-47 ran over to me; exhaling brandy fumes, he said, in quite good English, "Croatia soldier good. No kill. Only kill Chetniks (meaning the Serb population). In house any Chetniks?" He brushed past and went down to the shelter; I followed. He might have just murdered other old folk in the town, and in his drunken state, he might well do the same to the three old folks still sitting on hard chairs outside our radio room.

The soldier questioned them and then started to lift the old man up by his arm. I guessed he wanted to take him upstairs and most likely gun him down in the street. The old man and the two old ladies were mute, shaking with fear. I thought about my next move, as the old man gently resisted.

"No more Krajina. No more Chetniks!" Not wanting to waste any more raping, looting and killing time, he left. I followed him back up the stairs as he left the premises then went to the front of the house to try to get a few more sandbags around the top of the bunker. In short order, I ran back in as a T-55 battle tank came roaring down our street, loaded with young Rambo lookalikes wearing camouflage bandanas and firing their assault rifles in all directions.

In the bunker during Oluja, 1995

Later that day, as I wrote about the event in my journal, my heart rate went up just thinking about it. Although the T-55 main battle tank was first deployed in 1949, with 86,000 produced, it remained a fearsome weapon of war. It fires four 100-millimetre rounds per minute, holds a crew of four and has a top speed of forty-eight kilometres per hour. At least fifty armies worldwide retain this formidable tank in their arsenal.

Back in the shelter, all we could do was sit and listen to the radio chatter, answer requests for information from Zagreb and wait for more intrusions. I thought about the trip we made out of town with the truckload of people. It seemed like it had happened days ago. Recalling it made me sweat all over again; very scary. Outside, over the radio traffic noise and the generator roar, small-arms fire could be clearly heard.

August 6th

The second phase of the battle for Knin had started. When our night guard, Tommy and I were building up the sandbagging on the front of the delegation, Emma, Claire and Sara were busy carrying down the rest of the computers, printers and sensitive files to keep them out of the hands of looters. As well, Emma had emptied the safe. Delegations carried enough cash to pay for the day-to-day needs, including food, electricity and wages for the local staff. As a convoyer, one of my duties each week was to collect a large bag of used currency from the Split delegation and deliver the cash to the delegations on my route into and out of the war zones. Some weeks I would have in excess of 100,000 DM stuffed under my seat, the equivalent of 60,000 USD. At the time, this was the way to keep the ICRC operations going.

The Yugoslav dinar was almost worthless due to rampant inflation. The self-proclaimed republic of Serbian Krajina issued the Krajina dinar, which proved to be totally without value. After the shelling stopped, I found a vast amount of this currency just blowing around like tickertape in the streets. One banknote I picked up had a face value of 500 million dinar.

Emma had parcelled up the delegation cash into six equal amounts; each of us had an envelope in our pockets with the sixth envelope in a petty cash tin ready to hand over as we expected to be robbed soon by the rear-echelon soldiers. The frontline troops overall acted in a somewhat professional manner as they had one goal in mind: to rid the Krajina of ARSK occupation. As the frontline troops moved out of the conquered areas to continue the fight, the second-rate occupation troops moved in and stayed. The looting was something to see. Everything was either smashed to pieces, burnt, thrown out onto the street or carted away.

The old man and his wife decided it would be safer to try to make the hazardous journey to the UN camp at the south end of Knin. That left the second old lady with us in her Sunday best, looking confused. Sara spoke to her and reassured her that everything was going to be OK.

Day 3 – first time out of the bunker – 1995

Emma asked Sara, Tommy and me to walk to the warehouse and bring the medical Cruiser back with the MAN truck before we lost those to the soldiers. If we thought the situation was secure, we should try to get to the hospital with some of the remaining medical supplies. We donned our helmets and flak jackets, topped by Red Cross bibs. It was 2 p.m., and for the first time since my excursion to Zrmanja, we were outside and totally exposed. I am hard-pressed to describe the feeling of vulnerability as we walked down the middle of the street that August afternoon. The walk to the warehouse would take forty minutes; we went three abreast, focused on avoiding the rubble, broken glass and discarded belongings. We skirted the occasional still smouldering, over-turned car in our path. We heard shooting, but in another part of town. We walked past a bar where the curtains blew in the warm breeze through the shattered windows. To my dismay, the front yard was full of soldiers on plastic chairs, diligently consuming cases of the local beer. As we walked by, they good-naturedly called us over for a drink, but we waved, smiled and walked on. We were not about to celebrate what had and was still happening to the population. It was not our war, only theirs.

A little farther on, we came across the ARSK troop carrier Mario, Melina and I negotiated round when we screamed through the shelling and mayhem on that first day. The diesel fire had burnt itself out along with anything else flammable; the large off-road tires, still smouldering, added to the smoke hanging around the town.

Once I opened the warehouse doors, I was able to get a better look at the damage from the direct hit. Cooking oil from the food parcels had soaked through much of the supplies. But there would be time later to sort out the mess. Our priority was to get to the hospital with supplies. Sara's medical Cruiser now had a puncture, and a hole in the windscreen made by a piece of shrapnel, half melted onto the dashboard. The Scania was missing its battery but looked OK otherwise; my lovely old Volvo water truck had a few more holes in the cab. While Tommy changed the puncture on the Cruiser, Sara and I quickly loaded the medical goods she thought they would need at the hospital. We locked the warehouse doors and left. In the MAN, I followed Sara and Tommy towards the hospital. Ten minutes later, we came across a hastily erected roadblock and we negotiated with the nervous soldiers for at least thirty minutes to no avail. They had orders not to let anyone through to the hospital. No reason.

After turning back, I noticed a row of five or six Lada and Yugo cars, a common vehicle on the roads of Yugoslavia. All had been crushed lengthwise by what must have been a tank. I wondered why the owners had not taken them when the town's population evacuated. They probably had no fuel.

Out of sight of the roadblock, Sara pulled over. We decided to try to get to the hospital by a back route we both knew. We didn't use the VHF to notify Emma at the delegation because the military monitored it. Using the back-door route, we arrived at the rear entrance to the hospital and it looked as if the building had been spared any serious damage. (We later learned that the hospital had received hits from two 120-millimetre shells.) Before the Croatian Army entered the town, the Canadian UNPROFOR went to the hospital and took thirty-five badly wounded Serbian persons, including "our" patient Josip, back to the makeshift hospital at the UN base. Many dead bodies were noted in the town at that time.

I had been to the hospital many times delivering supplies and knew my way around. This time, entering with Sara, it felt totally different. We left Tommy at the loading dock. Our voices echoed in the gloomy, deserted corridors.

"Hello, is anyone here?" No response. Just the sound of a dripping tap.

All we found were soiled bandages, bed sheets and other medical stuff scattered across the wet floor by the reception area. I was worried what we might discover as we climbed the stairs and called out. Still, nobody around.

We looked in all the wards and found no one. We noted plenty of evidence of a hurried evacuation, chairs knocked over, broken glass and discarded pieces of clothing. As we started up to the fourth and last floor, we heard muffled voices in one of the wards. Nervously, we pushed open the double doors and were met with frightened stares from the few nurses and doctors standing there with perhaps twenty patients in their beds. I was impressed by the bravery of the medical staff in deciding not to flee with the rest of the population. They were relieved to see Sara and informed us that they had plenty of supplies as we, the Red Cross, had recently made a delivery. So, we decided to go to the UN camp on the other side of town to see if supplies were needed there. We thought that the makeshift hospital would be overwhelmed with the wounded. Walking back through the silence and gloom of the empty hospital, I wondered where all the former patients, there before the fighting started, had gone.

Tommy was visibly relieved to see us return to the loading dock.

I couldn't understand why we had not seen evidence of a UN presence in the town. As we crossed the bridge and approached the UN camp, the reason became obvious. Two T-55 battle tanks, parked with their main guns lowered and pointing menacingly, blocked the only gate in and out of the camp. It was abundantly clear that the Croatian military were going to finish this operation with no interference from the UN. We parked both vehicles away from the hulking monsters and walked up to the main gate. A few frightened people were entering the camp on foot, and we saw only UN soldiers on duty at the main gate behind their white-painted, sandbagged enclosure. We learned that four hours earlier, the camp had received a direct hit that killed seven civilians and wounded many more.

One of the tank commanders climbed down; we said we wanted to enter the camp and deliver medicines to the hospital. After some debate, with a roar and a very large cloud of diesel fumes, he moved away just enough to allow our Cruiser and truck to squeeze past.

The parade ground and the few vacant buildings were occupied by 700 civilians seeking safety. Many children and old folk were standing around with their laundry drying on the camp's barbed-wire perimeter. Negotiating the throngs of people, we came to the rear of the hospital and unloaded the boxes of medical supplies to the grateful, exhausted UN medical staff.

Sara left to find Canadian Major-General Alain Forand and Chief of Staff Colonel Andrew Leslie, so Tommy and I walked to the front of the hospital to offer our assistance. On entering, I was shocked by the scene in front of me. Family members attended to some, the few medical staff handled others, but many people were just lying on the bare wooden floor. The smell, the noise and shouting were too much for me. I saw a frail woman on the floor alone; I found a small thin mattress and lifted her onto it. Then I went outside for some air to stop my head from spinning. I've never been good in hospitals. Tommy came out a good hour later and found me outside, still unable to go back into the bedlam. All this time I was wearing my helmet and flak jacket; I felt safer keeping the gear on despite the thirty-degree temperature.

After Sara finished her meeting, the tank at the gate once more moved aside to let us out. We drove back in the dark, amid sporadic small-arms fire, the town illuminated by burning buildings. We parked both vehicles and trooped happily back into the shelter. Emma congratulated us on the afternoon's work, we all helped to cook a ration-pack curry, and each drank a shot of Rakia.

At 9 p.m., it was pitch-dark; judging by the amount of gunfire, the Croatians were just beginning to warm up. The AK-47 assault rifle held a magazine capacity of thirty rounds, and there didn't appear to be a shortage of ammunition. Half an hour later, we saw two soldiers standing at the bottom of the stairs. One was an officer and the other looked like his bodyguard. Both were wearing brand-new American Army combat fatigues. When they entered the radio room, we stood up and said hello.

"What is happening?" Emma asked. "Are you able to inform your military command of our whereabouts and afford us protection from drunken soldiers?"

I was relieved to at last see an officer. He explained that he would make sure we were not bothered anymore and would put a permanent Croatian police guard outside the delegation in the morning. Tommy, just woken up from a nap, jumped up and started handing out Emma's cigarettes. They looked a little bemused as they accepted the smokes. During this exchange, I saw how they were both staring at Sara and Emma. Claire had by this time sat back down to attend to the radio. Knowing the brutal history of this four-year-old war regarding rape and murder, I realized there and then that I was totally in love with Sara and would not allow anything to happen to her or indeed to any of the women.

Emma asked the officer when it might be safe to walk to her residence and see if her Toyota Corolla was still in the garage.

Four of the five Knin team, August 1995

"Not tonight," he replied. "There are still small pockets of resistance in the town that we are trying to clear out, but I will come back tomorrow before noon and escort you."

Then, to our great relief, they left and drove away in a typical Soviet-style Jeep, the UAZ-469, a vehicle similar to the Land Rover or the Toyota Land Cruiser but rather less sophisticated.

It was now 2 a.m., and we decided to try and get some sleep. It was a peaceful night in the radio room but not outside. Still, lots of small-arms fire, explosions, shouts and vehicles roaring around the town. Thankfully, we had no visitors during the night. Each of us had a thin mattress on the floor. Emma, as the boss, slept on the couch, and she told us she was still awake at three, watching the cockroaches run around, often over our sleeping forms.

August 7th

We were wide awake at 5:30 a.m., hoping to be able to get out and start work. Claire found some muesli, Tommy had a carton of long-life milk, I made tea and we had a rather pleasant breakfast. Afterwards, Tommy and I took the opportunity to haul the bloodstained mattress outside. As we propped it against the side of the house, we noticed two young soldiers riding a stolen motorbike and firing shots into the air.

The same Croatian liaison officer returned and let us know that we were the only humanitarian aid organization to stay during the attack, and we were to have unrestricted access to Croatian General Ivan Čermak and Canadian Major General Forand. Also, we were to have unrestricted access to all areas of what had been, until three days previous, the territory of the Republik Srpska Krajina, now Croatia. He then asked if we wanted him to escort us to Emma's residence. We explained that as the Red Cross, we could not be seen in the company of anyone carrying a weapon. He replied that he knew the Geneva Conventions; he would walk ahead, and we would follow at a distance. It was rather odd following this soldier along the now quiet and deserted streets of Knin.

One look at Emma's house was enough to tell us we would find no Corolla in the burnt-out garage. Most likely, it was well into Serbian territory, and we would not see it again. Thirty-five minutes later, after we thanked the officer back at the delegation, the Croatian police guard pulled up. Two large, sweaty police officers climbed out of their vehicle and, without saying a word to us, sat down on fold-up deck chairs in front of the main door; each lit a smoke. Seeing they were both carrying rifles and sidearms, Emma asked them if they would be so kind as to move away from the delegation and set up camp across the road. They did so reluctantly, explaining there was no shade across the road.

"While you were gone," Sara said, "we had a message from Zagreb giving us the green light to go out to work." The first thing I did was hang a large Red Cross flag on the side of the MAN truck parked outside. Then, in Sara's Cruiser Tommy and I drove over to the warehouse to assess the situation. En route, we saw many soldiers looting anything they could lay their hands on. Some buildings were still burning, but we heard just the occasional burst of gunfire. Soldiers were more intent on stealing than shooting. We were happy to see the doors of the warehouse intact. Inside, stepping over the mess of the shell-damaged individual parcels, I went to see if our fuel supply was intact. To my relief, it was. During the following weeks, with the looting becoming more and more brazen, our fuel supply was never discovered because inside the warehouse, we had built an area small enough to hold fifteen 200-litre drums of diesel and one 200-litre drum of petrol. The door to this area was not noticeable; at a distance, it looked like part of the wall.

As Tommy checked our other supplies for shell damage, I filled the Cruiser with fuel and put four jerrycans in the rear of the truck to take back to the delegation. Our supply of blankets, tents, water bladders, tarps, personal hygiene kits and Sara's medical stores were largely intact. Locking the warehouse doors, I noticed a small three-tonne truck with Split registration plates parked outside the warehouse next door. I knew he wasn't there to deliver stuff, so I got one of the large Red Cross stickers we used for the vehicles and stuck it above the others on the door in the hopes that it might deter any thieving of our supplies.

On the way back, I suggested to Tommy that we quickly call into our residence and retrieve the rest of my stuff. Both upper floors had been smashed and looted; it appeared that Croatian soldiers had stayed in our place for a couple of days, judging by the half-opened Croatian ration packs strewn around. The Croatian ration packs were the best, with chocolate, chewing gum, cigarettes and tasty food, all inside a handy cardboard carton. During their brief stay, they walked on all the bedding, poured cooking oil, and anything else we had in the fridge and cupboards over everything and smashed any glass in the apartment except the windows. A disgusting mess. My room had received the same treatment as Sara's and Claire's. Also, I had all my stuff stolen: convoy running money, some clothing and a good pair of winter boots. I was happy I'd rescued my journals and bike earlier.

We still had the original old lady with us. As things were much quieter now, she said she would return to her small house, a five-minute walk away. An hour later, she was back, distraught, saying the soldiers had torn off her front door and smashed everything inside the house. She was seventy-five, and I suspect had very few possessions. I walked back down with her to see what I could do. Walking ahead of her through the wrecked door, I looked around and felt my anger rise. Brave young soldiers had pushed over the only piece of nice furniture she had, a display cabinet with ornaments and keepsakes. Everything was smashed. She told me these same two warriors had knocked her down, put a pistol to her head and threatened to shoot her. They were still outside roaring up and down the street in a stolen car. We walked back to the delegation with her in tears, where she laid down on her mattress in the medical storeroom and stayed there for the rest of the day.

Zagreb notified us that there were three busloads of displaced Serbian elderly folks and a few families on their way to Knin from other parts of the Krajinas. They would be with us in an hour and would be deposited at the school gym. Sara collected the medical supplies she needed while Tommy and I went back to the warehouse and loaded individual food parcels that were not too badly damaged.

On the way, I saw an old lady sitting on a concrete step in the ruins of a burnt-out shop. I wondered what she was doing there but had no time to stop. After loading the supplies, I had a close look at the water tanker; it seemed to be undamaged and still full of potable water. When we arrived at the school, a fifteen-minute drive away, displaced persons were already crowding into the gym; mostly old and infirm people, and a few children, sat on the floor. The few chairs had been taken by the more able-bodied. We handed out the food parcels but, due to the chaos, some got nothing. Tommy and I dragged in a bale of blankets to hand out to those who seemed to have the least. We were shoved aside, and the blankets quickly disappeared. We were glad to get outside and breathe some fresh air. The temperature in the gym was probably thirty degrees, and there was no available water as the town's supply was still cut off.

Leaving Tommy back at the warehouse to help Sara with the medical supplies, I went to see if I could get the water tanker running. Luckily, the Volvo still had a battery and started just fine. The Croatian police guarding the people at the school asked me to park the tanker at the front entrance so they could monitor the usage. On the way back to collect my truck, I again saw the old lady sitting on her stoop.

Two days later, I passed her again, stopped and gave her a bottle of water. I opened a cold curried chicken ration pack and put it in her hands. She was in shock; she looked at me blankly and tried to suck the spoon. I hated to leave her, but we had so much to do; the population at the UN camp was growing. Every hour, more people emerged from their basements asking us for help, and we told them to go to the UN camp. Our workload over the next few weeks was almost overwhelming – workdays of eighteen hours or more.

One elderly woman asked me to look at an unexploded rocket lodged in her garden amongst her flowers and vegetables. I was horrified to see her picking a bunch of flowers around the one-and-a-half-metre-long silver rocket. I warned her to keep away and said I would inform the UN bomb disposal team. She insisted I take the flowers to the delegation. Her simple act of kindness amid murder and mayhem almost brought me to tears.

A couple of days later, the new Croatian authorities arranged to have the school gym residents taken across the front lines and into Serbia. This freed up my water tanker, and as it was still three-quarters full (the police must have monitored the water usage a little too well), I parked it at the delegation. At the rear of the tank, Tommy and I built a shower cubicle out of wooden pallets and took turns having our first real wash in a week. The women were uncomfortable showering outside and wisely decided not to take advantage of it.

The water we had stored in the generator room was almost too hot to touch, so I hooked up a length of rubber hose to one of the water tanks, wedged it into the floor joists and voila, an inside shower! Sara, Emma and Claire took turns having a very hot shower. The water simply drained away through the dirt floor.

Each morning, we saw the tanker water level had gone down. Our police guard reported that after dark, many people came and took water back to their homes. I was happy about this but knew we had no way of refilling it as the town's main water supply had not yet been repaired. As well, the generator was still going flat out, and the engine oil was almost gone. I made a mental note to ask at the UN vehicle pool for a gallon or two.

Sara and General Forand had agreed to establish a radio link between the delegation and the UN, who were still confined to the camp; when they received requests for help, they would call us to see if we could deal with it.

The old lady who had been staying with us decided she too would walk to the UN camp. I went upstairs with her to the front door and gave her the fifty DM note I had in my pocket. I watched her slowly walk up the road in her best clothes to a life of uncertainty as a displaced person in her own town.

Later in the afternoon, we received a call from the UN asking if we had any tents. As Tommy and I drove to the warehouse, we discovered that the Scania had been stolen. Its battery had been taken a few days before and, therefore, I had thought the truck would be safe. We found fifteen medium-sized tents and, at the back of the warehouse, a very large tent, which we struggled to load. One tank at the camp gate moved a few yards and let us through. With help from some of the displaced men, we soon had the tents set up on the remaining open area.

As we were leaving, a UN soldier told me we could go to the camp's bakery once a day for a loaf of bread. Tommy jumped out and came straight back with a loaf of warm bread that smelled simply delicious. Back at the delegation, Sara and Claire had warmed up a ration-pack dinner and were over the moon to see the fresh bread to go with it. After I'd eaten and had a glass of Rakia, I filled up the generator with diesel, remembering I had forgotten to ask at the UN camp for oil.

It was 12:30 a.m. and we had been working for nineteen hours. As I dropped off, I noticed the only sound was that of the generator.

August 8th

Finally, the UN personnel were able to leave the camp. It seemed the Croatians had finished their nefarious work and moved the two battle tanks from the main gate. Sara and Claire decided it was a good day to establish a working relationship with the Croatian police at the Knin Police station, a legitimate target yet left intact during the shelling. We drove there with Sara behind the wheel. At the main junction in the town centre, we were stopped by military police and saw four T-55 battle tanks, several APCs and Jeeps, and trucks full of young bandana-wearing soldiers sat idling, waiting to move out towards the fighting. A poignant reminder that we were in the middle of a war. After a few minutes, a cameraman from the Belgian National News Agency shoved his lens at me, and the reporter with him started questioning me. I was more interested in watching the troops starting to pull out. Three of the tanks left in a cloud of diesel smoke; the fourth tank showed off by pirouetting, then tearing up the soft asphalt before following the others. I did not respond to the reporter's questions, in order to maintain neutrality.

"Have you witnessed any atrocities?"

"Have you seen many dead bodies?"

"What is the situation in the local prison?"

I knew better than to respond.

After the third, "Sorry I can't answer that," the journalist stepped back onto the sidewalk, just as the MPs waved us on.

It was another hot, sunny day. We stood on the front steps of the police station, waiting for the chief to arrive, and talking to his deputy. We wanted the lists of and access to the prisoners they had. I mentioned that our Scania had been stolen the day before. We knew that Croatian police were subservient to the Croatian military (who we suspected of stealing my truck); they would not be interested in finding the truck as they were busy with their own style of policing.

Having been around Scanias a lot, I knew their engine sound and as I heard the distinctive hollow roar, I looked, and around the corner saw my truck, flat out in low range, doing twenty kilometres an hour. It was loaded with soldiers waving their weapons and singing, all very jolly and probably all full of Rakia, celebrating the

Croatian victory. I pointed to the truck and asked the deputy police chief to kindly send an officer to retrieve it. He shrugged. The chief arrived; Sara and Claire followed both men inside.

While I was waiting, I saw two handcuffed and bedraggled ARSK POWs frogmarched into the police station. An hour later, Sara and I dropped Claire off at the delegation and went to the warehouse to check for any further looting. As we pulled up, we saw a Croatian Army ambulance parked in front of the main door. They had broken the chain on the door and were almost finished stealing as many medical goods as they could cram into their vehicle. Pulling in front of the ambulance to block their way, Sara and I confronted the two soldiers. Sara was not going to allow this theft. At first, they tried to justify their actions, but Sara stood with arms crossed, while saying out of the corner of her mouth, "And please don't help them Roger.", instructed them to put everything back, *immediately*. To my surprise, they did, sheepishly. Sara said they would have to answer to General Čermak himself for the theft. We knew our medical goods would have ended up on the black market within a day or two. Once we were sure they'd left, we headed off to ask General Čermak for a police guard at our warehouse. He said there would be a police presence there that day.

On the way back through town, Sara said nonchalantly, "There is your Scania." It was parked outside a soldier-packed bar. As Sara pulled up, I jumped out and hurried across to the bar. I had the key in my pocket, but as the truck was stuck in low range, I was certain it had been hot-wired. Climbing into the cab, shaking like a leaf, I squatted down underneath the steering wheel, felt around and found the ignition wires. It took a few tries before the ignition light came on, then a few more tries before the starter motor light flashed on. I touched the wires together, and the motor burst into life with a roar that could be heard in the bar.

I expected a soldier to come running out and confront me, but there was no reaction. I jumped into the driver's seat and took off flat out at twenty kilometres an hour to the UN base where I could safely leave my Scania at the motor pool, and maybe get some generator oil at the same time.

As I drove down the street, I half expected to get shot at. Fifteen minutes later, I was at the UN gates, yelling at the soldiers to let me in pronto. With the barrier lifted I went straight to the rear of the camp to the motor pool. Seeing the South African sergeant there, I breathlessly told him that I had just stolen my truck back.

"Could I leave it here for a while?"

"Yes," he said, slapping me on the back. "Good man. We need more men like you!"

Fifteen minutes later, Sara collected me, and we drove back to the delegation, still feeling a little nervous. Later that day, we received a call from General Čermak's aide asking why we took the Scania. He said they had confiscated it and were about to call us to come and pick it up. We had a chuckle while I tried to calm down from my unnecessary bravado.

Seven soldiers from the Nigerian UN troops offered to help clean up the mess in the warehouse. While they were busy inside, Tommy and I borrowed a ladder, a large tarp and some two-by-four lumber from another warehouse and tried to patch up the hole in the roof. It was ready to collapse at any moment, so we didn't spend long up there.

Later that morning, we thanked the troops for their assistance, and they drove away in their truck. Two minutes later, Sara, who was just in front of the Nigerians on her way to the warehouse, saw the truck driver misjudge the width of the bridge over a small river on the way back to the camp. It rolled over and landed upside down on the riverbank. We grabbed a stretcher from the warehouse and ran the 200 yards. Six of the soldiers had scrambled back up and were sitting there, shocked and bruised. One man was missing. Tommy and I looked inside the upside-down cab and saw the seventh soldier jammed up against the windscreen, unconscious. I reached in, untangled him from his rifle and handed it to Tommy. We managed to pull him out, put him on the stretcher and lay him on the bank. Sara examined him for head and spinal cord injuries. Minutes later, he came around, and another UN truck pulled up and took them all back to the base.

Direct hit on ICRC Knin warehouse, 1995

At noon, Sara and I went to the hospital, now filled with injured and shocked civilians. We gave each of them a Red Cross Message form and took down their names.

In the four years of the conflict, the tracing department had processed over eighteen million messages, visited 54,000 detainees in 520 makeshift prisons and holding centres, and reunited 4,500 families. This number was second only to the work of the ICRC during the Second World War.

The Red Cross Message form was a single sheet with the sender's name, the recipient's name and just twenty-three lines for a message. Each form was then collected, returned to the tracing office and read by a team of trained staff to ensure it did not contain anything of military or political sensitivity. Then the names were entered into a large database, and the process of trying to reconnect families started. Refugees from conflicts worldwide as far back as the Franco-Prussian War in 1870 had been and continue to be reunited. It is a time-consuming process.

I was moved by giving out the forms and trying to lend support to the lost and frightened people we encountered. After a couple of hectic hours, we headed back to the delegation with the first of many sacks of mail. The mail would go to Split to be processed, at least until Knin had the staff to deal with the volume.

It was 8 p.m. when I dropped Sara at the delegation to begin her detailed daily reports for Zagreb and Geneva. I headed out to the UN camp to pick up a loaf of bread for dinner. Although some houses were still smouldering, the fires had mostly gone out. With my fresh loaf of bread on the passenger seat, about halfway home on the main street, a man came running out of a side street, jumped in front of my Cruiser and started banging on the bonnet.

I recognized him as an Englishman from the UN Canbat. I never really knew what his work was, but it involved travelling around the Krajinas. He screamed at me to drive my Cruiser up the street he'd run out of, waving for me to follow. Just three metres off the main street, he pointed to a group of Croatian soldiers aiming their weapons at a terrified young man cowering against a wall.

The UN guy told me he had thought it was safe to go out to work with his field officer. I surmised that the soldiers had probably been drinking for the last six hours and were not in any mood to see a UN vehicle, especially one containing a Serb male passenger. They had dragged the field officer out of the vehicle and were preparing to shoot him. My vehicle was unmistakable, with a large Red Cross flag flying from the rear door. The UN guy begged me to stay and just observe. He reasoned the soldiers wouldn't shoot if they were being watched by a Red Cross official. I explained the situation to Emma over the VHF, who advised me to leave the scene and return to the delegation. I told her if I did, the poor guy would be killed.

Watching the scene from my vehicle, I wondered what to do if they did kill him. After twenty minutes of sheer tension and furious discussion, the soldiers pushed him back into the UN vehicle and walked off, looking for an easier target. Back at the delegation, Emma was pleased to see me with the bread, and back in one piece. Nothing was said about my decision to remain at the scene; however, Emma did report the incident to General Čermak.

Tommy and I cooked dinner and suggested to Emma that we eat upstairs. She was hesitant at first, but we all needed to get out of the radio room for a bit, so she agreed. We got some clean sheets from the medical stores and laid them on one of the office tables. With a few candles from a refugee pack burning, the five of us sat down and had a peaceful meal with warm champagne in coffee cups. A gentle evening breeze blew through the broken windows. We felt somewhat relaxed for the first time in days. There was very little gunfire outside, but we did sleep down in the shelter.

As we were still the only building in the whole of Knin with electricity, I was expecting more visitors in the night. In the morning, we noticed someone had been in the offices while we were sleeping. Whoever it was had put the office chairs in order, tidied the desks, stood up a filing cabinet toppled on its side and swept the floor. We looked at one another in surprise. We never did discover our night cleaner's identity; odd and lovely.

August 9th

Five a.m., almost daylight. I'd had five hours sleep and felt ready for what the day would bring. ICRC Zagreb had asked Emma to organize a public food kitchen. Many elderly inhabitants remained in Knin, and their numbers were growing with the addition of others from the surrounding villages who had no means of finding food. The military authorities had given us an abandoned restaurant on the main street, a short walk from our delegation. We then received a radio message from the Split delegation that they were sending two very welcome teams of local Red Cross personnel with three more Land Cruisers to help us. At 9 a.m., they found us down in the radio room. After a quick briefing, Tommy and I went to the restaurant; Sara and a newly arrived Swiss delegate went to speak with the military about stocking the kitchen.

There was no glass left in the restaurant windows, and most of the tables and chairs had either been broken or stolen. There was rotten food everywhere. The basement was half-full of sewage, with food and other material floating around in it. While Tommy and a helper were sorting out the mess upstairs, I took off my sandals, rolled up my jeans and, barefooted with a shovel and a bucket, started throwing the stuff out the back door. Not the best solution, but we needed to get the kitchen open and operational as soon as possible. After two hours, I had managed to get most of the floor fairly clean. In the thirty-degree temperature, things dried out quickly. Emma was not pleased that I had personally mucked out the basement, but she understood my decision that the job needed to be done, and I couldn't ask a labourer to do something I wouldn't.

Opening the two freezers, I almost fell over from the stench. They had been full of meat before the attack and had sat for a week in the heat. I knew the Croatian military had a sanitation squad in Knin whose job was to collect corpses and dead livestock in the interests of hygiene. I radioed in and asked to have the two freezers taken away. They came within the hour.

By this time, Tommy had sorted out the upstairs and put plastic sheeting over the broken windows. We went to collect the donated food and loaded two tonnes of tinned food by hand into the MAN, with help from three Croatian men recently arrived from a refugee camp on the Dalmatian coast. Back at the restaurant, with help from two more young men, we had the truck unloaded by noon. One of them tried to stuff cans of food into his trouser pants, and I made him return them. I was not going to allow theft to be part of the job. Later, as a thank you for their help, I did invite our five workers to take as many cans of food as they could carry. We could do no more with the kitchen until the authorities got water and electricity back into town. It was at least clean and ready.

During the next few weeks, thousands of Croatians expelled during the fighting three years previously, returned to either reclaim their property or, in many instances, take any vacant house as their own. One of my truck drivers, who had been living as a refugee for the past three years in Split, came back and found his house had been well looked after and the front yard full of washing machines and dryers, which he soon sold at a handsome profit. This was the exception rather than the rule. Most frequently, the returning population, ninety-nine percent Croatian, found their homes destroyed.

I received a radio message from the delegation asking that we load some flour that had just been discovered at a local school for delivery to the UN camp bakery. At the school, we found the flour hidden in a basement storeroom. The room was full of UNHCR-donated sacks that weighed thirty kilograms each. One volunteer on top of the pile passed each bag down to be carried up into the daylight and loaded into the back of my trusty MAN. Two hours later, after we had moved twenty-five percent of the bags, I noticed in the gloom a sleepy-looking soldier standing just inside the doorway. He said he'd been detailed to guard the flour.

"And don't take any more."

Then as an afterthought, he added, "Oh, they have been booby-trapped." He showed me a sign written on a piece of cardboard. PAZI MINIRANO!! We all knew this sign well. WARNING MINES!!

From 1991 to 1995, Bosnia and Herzegovina had some two million land mines scattered over two and a half percent of the country, making it one of the most land-mine-contaminated countries in the world. I told my guys not to touch anything else, and we walked quietly back upstairs. Outside in the sunshine, we all looked like we had seen a ghost. I was shaking, with cold sweat on my brow; how close we came to be being blown to bits, maybe with the very next bag lifted. I felt quite sick. When the ARSK realized they were going to have to leave South Krajina, they likely decided to booby-trap the flour, not giving a damn who was killed. Everyone in the whole of the former Yugoslavia was aware of the dangers of mines, booby traps and all sorts of unexploded ordnance. But hiding mines amongst flour bags takes a malicious mind indeed.

I kept thinking about our narrow escape on the drive to the UN camp. We were exhausted with the strain and long hours since the shelling had stopped. *Who expected danger lurking in even the most mundane of things, like a bag of bloody flour?* The bakery guys were happy for the flour we did manage to get.

After filling the generator with fuel and oil (I remembered to get some from the UN) and a very hot, muddy-feet shower, we sat down together for another ration-pack dinner, with the fresh UN bread and a can each of warm Croatian beer kindly provided by the Split team. We were still sleeping in the radio room. We had no faith in the occasional police presence across the road.

CHAPTER 13

Sector South

* * * * *

Prior to Operation Storm, our housekeeper Beljana would often cook and leave dinner for us. She lived five kilometres out of town and walked into work; someone would always give her a ride home.

Early one morning following Operation Storm, I decided to drive to Beljana's house in the hopes of finding her or at least finding out where she might have gone. Her door was unlocked so, after knocking and calling out, I walked in. I was happy to see that the house hadn't been looted or burnt out. Seeing her meagre belongings, I thought how lucky I was to be able to return to England and resume my life at the end of all this. Of Beljana there was no sign. I hoped she had made it safely to Serbia. The hamlet was deserted, and there was not a soul to be found. Peering into her cowshed, I found two young horned cows that had been chained up for many days waiting for her to milk them. That was not going to happen again in this barn. After struggling to unlock their chains and avoid their wicked horns, I managed to free them. Off they ambled down the deserted road. One small victory.

On the drive back to Knin, I came upon what looked like a woman wearing a fur coat, lying in the middle of the road. As it was early August and hot, I thought it very strange. Getting closer, I saw it was a large dog, shot dead, probably used as target practice by the Croatian soldiers. Coming from a small farming community myself, I found this quite distressing. I never really got used to seeing these innocent animals dead everywhere.

What first was, on August 1st, an assignment of a few days in Knin from ICRC Split, was becoming a permanent posting for me, and I couldn't have been happier. I thoroughly enjoyed all my assignments with the ICRC, and this final posting brought all my previous experiences into play. I took tremendous satisfaction from the work I was doing and the team I was working with.

I took on the field duties of an acting relief delegate and when the two tracing teams returned from Split the next day, I would have a translator to help me assess the food situation in the surrounding countryside and to find and register any of the remaining population. We suspected that the folks in the villages and hamlets had little idea of the general situation or how they could get help. This would free up Claire to pursue prison visits, tracing the growing flood of the displaced, and the expected thousands of Red Cross Messages.

August 10th

The Split teams arrived at 7:30 a.m. and reported no problems on the two-hour drive to Knin. I introduced myself to Mia, sat down with a map and explained the area we needed to cover each day. Mia had put her university studies on hold to gain some experience as a translator with the Red Cross. Before we left, I made sure we had flak jackets and helmets, both tanks full of fuel (giving the Land Cruiser an 800-kilometre range), some water, a medical kit, blankets, a clean ICRC flag, fully charged batteries for the radios and a stretcher (just in case). It had been five days since the shelling stopped. I hoped things would be reasonably secure outside of Knin. Still, best to be prepared and ready for the worst.

On the way out of town, I noticed many more voyeurs and returning people. I was disgusted by the notion of busloads of people on an excursion to see the aftermath of the attack. However, I came to realize that likely the tourists were once residents, or family members of former residents, driven out at the start of the war by the "rebel Serbs". I did know that some had come out of morbid curiosity, and later thought that they too must be extremely relieved that there was an end to the wars in their former country. There were also the mandatory occupation soldiers, still busy stealing everything not already stolen. One civilian guy passed us going the other way, presumably back to Split, perched on a small garden rotavator (the walk-behind sort) somehow hooked up to a tiny trailer with a cow standing serenely in the back.

Mia and I stopped at every undestroyed house; after honking the horn, we called out who we were and that we were there to help. Towards noon, we drove into Biskupija. In the village centre, a group of Croatian soldiers were sitting around the half-destroyed local bar, glaring at us as we drove by. Stopping the Cruiser, I felt a sinister atmosphere; I might have felt a little less nervous had an officer been present. It appeared, judging by the clothing and other household goods lying in the street, that the soldiers were taking a break from the hot, thirsty business of looting and terrorizing the few remaining old folks.

The sensible thing would have been to drive on. But we were there to find who was left in each village and protect the vulnerable. Tooting my horn, I drove round to the other side of the small village square, and in full glare of the bar denizens, tooted again and called out.

Mia spotted an elderly woman hobbling toward us, dressed in the traditional peasant garb of thick woollen stockings, thin black rubber slip-on shoes, a woollen sweater, headscarf and a clean flower-patterned blouse.

Greeting her, I used my limited Serbo-Croat, "*Dobar dan, kako ste?*" (Good day, how are you?)

She responded with "*Dobro. Hvala, kako ste vie?*" (Good. Thank you, and you?)

Although my language skills were improving each day, I didn't really understand what the approaching soldier, who seemed to be the gang leader, was shouting at me. Mia nervously translated. He was trying to intimidate us. He had lank, greasy hair, wore sweat-stained combat fatigues, and carried a large bowie knife on his belt, as well as the ubiquitous assault rifle with a spare thirty-round magazine taped to the weapon. As he repeated himself, I glimpsed a mouthful of black teeth. I tried not to recoil from the hot blast of his brandy-reeking breath. He demanded we leave *his* village.

"There is nothing here for you. Who do you think you are?"

Now, I don't take kindly to intimidation. Holding his baleful stare, I calmly explained who we were, what we were doing and what we would continue to do in the village. As Mia translated, I threw in a few Geneva Convention words for good measure. Then I turned my back on him and started to speak with the old lady, who seemed to be quite calm. We stood there, in the middle of that almost-deserted village in the hot sun, feeling the even hotter glare from the soldier.

With Mia translating, I asked the old lady, "Do you want to go somewhere private so we can talk freely?"

"Yes," she replied nervously.

We followed her to her squat, small, stone-built house, with the soldier tagging along. I presumed he wanted to make sure she did not tell us what really had been going on in her village. I stopped, spun around, looked him in the eye, and said that we would conduct our interview in private. It was a pure battle of wills. He was drunk, dirty, most probably guilty of the most unspeakable crimes and had a weapon. I, on the other hand, was sober, smartly dressed and instead of a Kalashnikov had the Red Cross emblem as my protection. After a few tense moments, he turned and walked back to the bar to continue his drinking. I was exhausted by the strain of the moment but happy to have laid down the ground rules, at least in this village.

When we sat down in her sparse kitchen, the elderly woman apologized for not having anything to give us to eat or drink, as was the custom. I asked if she had been threatened, what she felt comfortable telling us, what had happened to her relatives, her name, date of birth, the address of any relatives here or abroad.

"Would you like to write a Red Cross Message to someone?"

She answered as if the soldier had been standing beside her, but I knew there was much more she wanted to say. Just as we left, I touched her on the shoulder. Well, she was nowhere near as calm as she first appeared; she shook and sobbed. Mia and I helped her back into the kitchen and listened to her story. The soldiers were going from house to house, throwing anyone and anything outside, taking any valuables they could find. If there was nothing worth taking, they would smash and burn everything, go back drinking for a bit, then start on the next house. They used most of the abandoned livestock for target practice. She was alone, waiting in terror for the soldiers to visit her. We had been in this village for two hours, but she was the only person willing to come and speak to us. If there had been more people wanting to see us, we hoped they'd come to our Cruiser, parked in full view. But no one else came.

Many times, when I gave these folks a small bit of comfort, they went completely to pieces. I hoped the soldiers would now leave the place alone, if not for humanitarian reasons, then at least out of fear of being reported to their superiors. I didn't feel happy about leaving the vulnerable woman, but maybe the next village needed our presence more. Our assessment area that day was southeast of

Knin, rural with small farms scattered amongst the rolling foothills leading to the Dinaric Mountain range. The roads were metalled, some showing the distinct washboard patterns left by T-55 tank tracks, narrow and potholed due to lack of maintenance since the start of the war.

We saw lots of livestock, dead in the fields from shrapnel wounds or soldiers' bullets. In the heat of summer, the carcasses blew up with internal gases, then in two to three days, they deflated and shrivelled to skin and bone within a week.

At the next hamlet of Polača, a few houses were still somewhat intact; one still smouldered, possibly set on fire the previous day. I reminded Mia about the danger of mines, to walk on the road or well-trodden path and never to walk on the roadside verges or any ground that looked even slightly disturbed. A simple thing like an unopened cigarette pack, perhaps dropped by a passing soldier, could contain cigarettes or could blow your hand off. It was easy to become over-confident, and it was too late once you picked up that cigarette pack.

The previous year, I had delivered a convoy of seed potatoes to ICRC Zenica for spring planting. The next morning, the head of sub-delegation asked me to attend, with six Swiss delegates, a British Army mine awareness course. I sat in the front row, listening to the three Scottish soldiers explain about Improvised Explosive Devices (IEDs) and the many ways to disguise a bomb. I was fascinated to see the samples they brought. They had very strong Glaswegian accents that even I had trouble understanding. The three soldiers knew their stuff. I found it quite amusing to see the look on the Swiss delegates' faces as they tried to decipher their accents.

One of my most unnerving moments regarding landmines happened the previous summer. Marko, my field officer, knowing I was going on one of my regular trips into Sector South, asked me if I would drive by his family's house, abandoned by them during the ethnic cleansing of the Krajinas in the early part of the war. He asked me to see what condition their house was in. He and his family, like many other IDPs, hoped to return to their former home one day.

Having delivered my load of medical goods, I was keen to get back on the road to Split and maybe have time for a dip in the warm Adriatic before it got dark. But a detour off my field trip route to look at Marko's house, maybe take a photo for him, shouldn't take long. His directions were spot on. Through the overgrown bushes and trees, I could just make out the roofline and chimney. Judging by the overgrown track leading to the house (which should have given me a hint), no one had lived there since his family had fled two years previously.

Parking the truck in the road, I started to walk up to the house. The dried grass on the track was overgrown and the colour of hay. I walked closer to take my photo when a feeling of sheer dread came over me. I stopped dead in my tracks. There could well be mines planted in the track. Anti-personnel mines can be deployed on the surface or buried ten to twenty millimetres deep; foot pressure would activate them. I tried to calm down and think clearly.

Honestly, I was really worried about my chances of going back down the track without having my foot blown off, and I could not make out where I had just walked. *Hmm, I have no choice but to turn around and start walking back.* There was no way to see, after two years, where a mine had been planted. Every step back was scary, and I resisted the urge to run. It took me five minutes to walk up and twenty to walk back. Sitting in the truck with both feet intact, I again realized what a terrible weapon landmines were. Also, what a complete idiot I had been.

Stopping at the Serbian checkpoint, I happily guzzled the Rakia handed to me by the grinning, unshaven soldier on duty. I was waved through the UN barrier, and when the Croatian soldiers saw my Split registration plates at the last checkpoint, the barrier was raised and off I went.

I wasn't sure if it was the experience on the track to Marko's house or the Rakia I had consumed that made my legs wobbly. When Split radio called asking my present position, I realized I had forgotten to let them know I was passing into Croatian territory. The following morning, Marko sought me out and asked how his house was. I replied with a straight face that I was unable to get close due to the risk of walking on the unused track. I decided not to mention my poor decision.

After walking around Polača and finding no one, I decided to head back to Knin by another route and repeat the process. We drove on, not seeing another soul – only destroyed and smouldering houses. At the first undamaged farmhouse, we stopped and called out. Seeing the front door ajar, we approached. Peering into the gloom, I noticed some shadows and heard what sounded like feet shuffling on the flagstone floor. It seemed like a chair, or something was at the back of the door, stopping it from swinging fully open. Not knowing what or who might be behind the door, I shoved harder. The door flew open, letting the daylight flood in. I was mightily relieved when twenty sheep came bounding past me into the sunshine. We thought about getting their names and addresses, but were too slow.

We had water back in parts of the town, including our delegation, but not in the school where another three busloads of displaced persons had turned up. So, Tommy and I refilled the water tanker at the fire station and left it at the school.

Emma called a team meeting, and we discussed how we were individually coping and how we could support each other. The result was that we decided to sleep upstairs in the offices, to avoid the noise and heat in the shelter and to try to regain a semblance of normalcy. The situation at night in the town was a lot quieter, and we felt that it was safe. With the breeze blowing through the broken windows, our night was a bit eerie, but pleasantly cool.

August 11th

I felt good after sleeping for four and a half hours and although I wasn't sure how much longer I could function effectively on such scant amounts of sleep; adrenaline kept me going during the day. After a quick cup of tea, Tommy and I delivered food parcels and blankets to the 240 people in the school gym. The fitter ones lay on the few benches available while most had to make do with the wooden floor and if they were lucky, they had a coat to lie on. We left the supplies in one of the empty offices and gave the key to a member of the committee the refugees had formed. We asked that everything be distributed fairly. Normally, we would not have just left the supplies due to the risk of theft or unfair distribution, but we didn't have the time. I was interested to see how groups of people organized themselves and identified their leadership. The committee structure was an evident process to get people through difficult decisions.

Sara now had a field officer from Split, Ana, who had Croatian Red Cross experience. To have a field officer with some experience was very helpful, as you knew they understood the organization, and especially the principles.

The Red Cross staff I worked with across the former Yugoslavia – whether Croatian, Serbian or Bosnian – were amazing and lived the seven fundamental principles. They demonstrated their humanity and impartiality every day. For example, a new local staff member was sent to Knin from Split and was witnessed by another Croatian Red Cross staff member belittling some of the remaining Serb elderly, bragging about the Croatian victory; she was immediately dismissed.

When Mia and I headed out to the warehouse for fuel, I was relieved to find nothing burgled. Even at this early hour, several of the other small factories were being stripped of anything of perceived value. I had yet to notice the promised police presence at our warehouse.

Burning Serb houses in Sector South, 1995

We headed out towards the village of Cetina, near the Dinaric Mountains. We would start there and work our way back towards Knin. It was another beautiful August day in what was called Sector South, but I supposed should now be called Croatia. The farther we got from Knin, the more buildings were on fire. According to a security message from Zagreb, pockets of remaining Serb soldiers roamed the countryside, shooting at anything or anyone. It looked to me like the burning houses were Serb owned and abandoned in the exodus seven days before. Many of the houses had a Tetragrammaton cross daubed on the walls to identify them. Clearly, the ARSK did not want the conquering Croats to inhabit their homes, thus the burning of the houses. After two hours of driving slowly through the lovely countryside and not seeing another living soul, apart from a few Croatian soldiers, we came to Cetina, a village of twenty-five houses.

Before Operation Storm, there would have been 100 people living in Cetina. But now, there was just one old lady, standing in the middle of the road with her donkey tethered to another donkey, lying stone dead. We stopped to ask how she was, how her food situation was, and would she give us her name? She answered pleasantly enough.

I then realised the absurdity of the situation, interviewing this frail old lady in the summer heat, in the middle of the road, in the deserted village, with two donkeys present, one of them dead.

"Would you like me to pull the dead donkey off the road for you?" (Clearly, the one standing was not going to.)

"Yes, please."

I untied the rope from the very relieved living donkey, attached the dead one to the rear hitch on the Cruiser and dragged it to the side of the road. The smell was overwhelming. We moved to sit in the shade to see if she needed anything. She only wanted to know where and how her family were. All I could do was to get her particulars and ask her to fill out a Red Cross Message. She said she was OK for everything else; however, she was clearly in shock.

Several hours later, the road turned into a dirt track and ended. Turning around was tricky. I didn't want to drive on the verge because of the mine risk.

We drove slowly all day, tooting the horn, hoping to coax people out of hiding. Just as we were ready to head back, Mia said, "Stop, I think there is someone up in the woods." We both looked, remembering the warning that rogue bands of ARSK soldiers were wandering the countryside.

Slowly an old man appeared. When he saw who we were, he started to walk down towards us. His dishevelled appearance suggested he had been out in the woods for quite some time. Mia spoke to him quietly and slowly, as he seemed very nervous. After fifteen minutes, we saw two more old men coming toward us, in the same condition. I asked Mia to continue speaking with them gently while I stood and listened. I wanted them to see that we could be trusted.

Apparently, the three brothers fled their village on the first day of Operation Storm and had been hiding out in the woods for seven days, watching house after house being blown up, used for tank fire practice, or simply burnt to the ground. They had very little to drink and ate any food they could find in the many abandoned houses. After listening to their harrowing story, one of them showed me his broken finger and told me how painful it was. He thought I was a medic, a common assumption when people saw our Red Cross vehicle. People were a little disappointed when I explained I was not a doctor.

Opening my first aid kit, I dressed his finger with two small splints, wrapped it with gauze and tied it together with a lovely bow. With his gnarled hands, he took my head and, with tears in his eyes, kissed me on the forehead.

After getting their names and addresses and asking them to write a Red Cross Message, we gave them some bottled water and wished them good luck. They said they would make their way to Knin on foot.

I suggested that the gentleman with the broken finger try to get to the Knin hospital and have it looked at by a real doctor. He simply nodded.

★ ★ ★

The previous summer, I would sometimes drive down and park just inside the Split dock gates to see what ships had come in. There could be a UN, commercial or a private ship. I was always interested to see what flags they flew and where they were from. There was a Royal Navy fleet auxiliary ship in one time, unloading supplies for the British battalion. I asked permission to come on board and spent a pleasant hour chatting with the purser over a cup of real tea with real milk and a biscuit.

One day, I was inside the docks watching a Turkish military ship disembark a brand-new battalion to replace the one finishing their tour of duty in Central Bosnia. The temperature in Split at the time was in the thirties. I was wearing a T-shirt and shorts. The soldiers were wearing combat gear and carried a full pack, rifle, webbing, water bottle, ammunition pouches, a flak jacket and steel helmet, and their personal gear. I believe the helmets were steel as the Turkish military had not changed over to the lighter composite helmets that most foreign militaries serving under the UN umbrella had adopted.

I thought it amusing to see these guys totally ready for war in the Split docks. The war was a good day's drive from the docks, but I had to admit that, tooled up as they were, they looked organized, confident and impressive. As they walked down the steep gangplank and lined up on the dock in arrow-straight lines, one of them tripped and fell eight metres onto the dockside with a crash. The discipline was amazing; none looked when this soldier fell. Eyes front, nobody moved.

An officer came running over and, in English, asked me to help with the injured soldier. I thought it best not to tell him I was not a doctor. I knew our field nurse was at the hospital, a few minutes away. I told him to bring the soldier to my Cruiser and lay him in the back on a stretcher.

"Mary, Mary. Mary, this is Roger. Do you copy, over?" I was very happy when she immediately replied. I explained that I was at the docks with a Turkish soldier who seemed to have a head injury.

She said she'd meet me at the front entrance of the hospital. The unarmed English-speaking Turkish officer jumped in with me. Mary and a local doctor took the injured soldier straight into the emergency room. Three weeks later, he was reunited with his battalion, none the worse for wear. Even after the three-day training with the MASH in Zagreb, I was clearly not a proper doctor!

★ ★ ★

We kept driving slowly, tooting the horn, only finding smouldering buildings, stray animals grazing at the roadside and dead farm animals. Destroyed and abandoned houses' gardens were strewn with the personal possessions of their fleeing inhabitants; broken-down tractors and trailers, anything with wheels that the owners thought would carry them away from the approaching attack littered the verges. Every house, hamlet and village told the same sad story of fear. When we stopped and turned off the engine, the silence was complete but for the singing birds.

As we passed through yet another deserted village, I investigated an auto repair shop. The door was wide open, and, in the shadows, two large eyes stared out at me at ground level. Mia and I were edgy with lack of sleep and the summer heat in this eerily abandoned land. I was loathe to investigate these strange, staring eyes. Nevertheless, standing just inside the workshop door for a few moments to accustom my eyes to the gloom. I heard heavy breathing. Looking down into the inspection pit, I was shocked to see a cow looking at me with frightened bovine eyes. She would never get out of that pit without help from the fire brigade and some heavy equipment. The thought of what eventually happened to that poor animal bothered me for some time.

The Split team were waiting in their vehicles when we arrived back, anxious to leave before it got dark. We were working fifteen-hour days, and the team still had another two hours to go before they arrived home. I tried to get back from our patrols earlier from then on.

We were still sleeping upstairs. Our office windows were now covered with plastic sheeting, so anyone who wanted to climb in could, but I had managed to fix the front door a bit more securely.

Sara had been out in the field as much as Mia and me but had still managed to pick up a loaf of fresh bread. Tommy and Claire had cooked another delicious dinner. After a few weeks of eating ration packs, they all tasted the same, but we were lucky to have them. With the fresh bread, a glass of vino and good company, I honestly would not have wanted to be anywhere else.

That evening we received a radio message from Chris, an Englishman I had come to know well since beginning my mission. It was he who had asked me to check in on Vesna and her daughter when I was stationed in Belgrade, which seemed like a very long time ago.

Chris had been working in Zenica as a relief delegate, and he was getting married in two days' time to Dragana, who also worked for the ICRC as a local staff member. His radio message asked if one or two of us would like to attend their wedding in Zagreb. Emma suggested that Tommy and I go. The looting, burning and shooting had levelled off, and she could spare us for a couple of days. We said that Sara and Claire should go as we thought they needed a break more than we did. Our mumbled protests were dismissed.

Two days later, the Split team arrived, minus Mia who was also taking time off. They brought an extra driver to take us to the Split airport. Emma had given us both a new T-shirt from the stock we kept for displaced persons. We had nothing else to bring except ourselves. Tommy took the rear bench seat, and I sat in the front. It was wonderful just to sit there and stare out the window. It was the most relaxed I had been for some time.

Immediately, Tommy was fast asleep, and I was also out for the count. Two hours later, the driver shook my shoulder and informed us we were at the airport. Tommy had fallen off the bench. He was in such a deep sleep I had to shout to wake him up. The driver was anxious to get going and gave us our flight tickets, the cost of which would be deducted from our per diem allowance. As we walked to the passport control, I glanced at Tommy; he was in a state! When we left Knin, he had looked fairly presentable, wearing the clean T-shirt. After rolling around on the floor in the back of the Cruiser for two hours, he looked like a coal miner: all grey and grubby, hair plastered down one side of his face, bloodshot eyes and stumbling. I was exactly the same, minus the grey and grubby part.

The plane was a standard no-frills Boeing 737. Waiting to taxi out felt wonderful. The thought of flying 20,000 feet through the clouds and away from the war, even if for a couple of days, was hard to describe. The next thing I heard was one of the cabin crew telling me it was time to disembark. Of the one-hour flight and landing, I could remember absolutely nothing.

★ ★ ★

When I was a seven-year-old boy growing up in Wanborough, a small village situated along a Roman road in southern England, I would catch the local bus the five miles into the town of Swindon to spend Saturdays with my nan. Percy Chaney was the owner-driver of the bus and lived in the village. He knew and cared about everyone. Every Saturday morning at ten, the bus would leave Wanborough, picking up people along the way. It returned from Swindon at four in the afternoon. I was often the first on and the last to get off. In the summer months, with the chrome ashtrays and the intoxicating aroma of cigarette butts and warm dust the worn blue velour seats gave off, I would doze off to the lullaby of the wheel bearings and the gentle whine of the old gearbox. After all the passengers had left and we got to my stop, Percy would walk to the back of the bus, shake my shoulder and, in his strong Wiltshire accent say, "Come on, Roger. It's time to get off."

I caught Percy Chaney's bus for many years, until my dad decided to buy a car for the family. His motorbike was still the way he got to and from work, but on weekends the car would be carefully removed from the garage, polished and off we would go for a spin. Percy was not pleased about this. I suppose he could see a time when more and more people owned a car and he would lose his business, as eventually he did. The Queen of the Hills Coach Company closed a few years later.

★ ★ ★

When the flight attendant shook my shoulder, that's where I was, asleep with the sun on my face in the back of Percy Chaney's bus. It took Tommy and me a few moments to realise where we were. The security control officer waved us through when he saw our ICRC passes. Outside, we were about to call the delegation and ask for a driver to come and pick us up when along came a Cruiser thoughtfully sent by Chris. The drive from the airport took forty-five minutes, and we were once again fast asleep until the driver woke us up. The Welcome Desk arranged for the driver to take us directly to the Irish Embassy. It wasn't really the Irish Embassy; rather, it was the house where the four Irish Red Cross convoy drivers lived. Two had been sent to Rwanda, and the other two guys were on standby to go as well.

Tommy and I each found a bed and fell into it. Later in the evening, I heard the bedroom door open, and someone say, "Hey, there's somebody in my bed!" Another voice said, "Leave him alone. The two of them have just flown up from Knin for Chris' wedding." We slept for sixteen hours; towards noon, Chris called and said a driver would come and pick us up at two.

Tommy and I drank copious amounts of Croatian beer at the reception and stayed up all that night with Chris, Dragana and the best man and his girlfriend. I remembered very little of the actual wedding ceremony. The next thing I recalled was flying through the early-morning streets of Zagreb in the best man's car on the way to the airport; he drove one-handed, firing his pistol through the sunroof in celebration. So much for the no weapons rule.

August 14th

An hour later, with a bump and squeal of tires, we landed in Split. After a quick hello at the delegation, we welcomed a cup of coffee to offset our pounding hangovers. We were driven back through what had been, before Operation Storm, the front lines. On the trip back to Knin, the still-smouldering buildings and desolate countryside brought us back to the current reality.

Sara and Ana were out working in the field. We now had a young, experienced guy from Sarajevo to monitor the constant radio traffic, leaving Emma free to support the two tracing teams that had been deployed from Zagreb. The teams found accommodation in Knin for the next two months and would be needed to complete the tracing work. Weekends, they returned to Zagreb for a break, then came back to Knin for another gruelling week.

Oluja – aftermath Knin, 1995 (courtesy of alamy.com)

The situation in the town was more chaotic than when we had left, just two days previously. The shooting during the day had stopped, but it was still dangerous to be outside during the darkness. More former residents returned to reclaim their houses, farms and apartments. They threw all the previous occupant's belongings outside.

Walking in town involved a degree of risk; you could be crushed under a couch thrown from a sixth-floor apartment window. *How ironic would the Wiltshire newspaper headline be? Local man killed by falling couch after the attack!*

Not all people moving back in were former owners. Many were displaced people from other parts of the Krajinas who simply decided they liked the look of a house or apartment and moved in. And of course, there were the ever-present, opportunistic looters.

Standing on the delegation front steps, I saw a rear-echelon Croatian soldier wearing runners trudge past, his assault rifle hanging across his back, struggling to carry all his loot. Stopping, he glanced at me and, without a word or the slightest air of embarrassment, tried to rearrange the guitar, suitcase, chainsaw and set of golf clubs he had just stolen. After realising he had to leave something behind, he threw the guitar down and off he walked.

That day, we moved into one of our former transit residences. The original owners had reclaimed their house, moved into one of the bedrooms and wanted to re-rent us the rest of the house. There was still little power in the town, so Tommy and I set up one of our small emergency generators on the rear balcony. We arranged one outlet for the single-ring burner (from the bunker) and two lights for us to use. Then, we ran one light into where the owners were living. The five of us were excited to be out of the bunker. Most of the windows in the new accommodation were still intact. We each had our own bedroom and some privacy, except Tommy, who slept in the living room and presented an obstacle to me sneaking into Sara's room in the middle of the night. We were still working long days, and although it was difficult staying awake until everyone else had gone to sleep, Sara and I managed to continue our affair. During working hours, we were professionals, but at night we were simply two people in love.

Emma asked why there was a light going into the owner's bedroom, and I responded that I had connected it as a courtesy. To be seen as totally impartial and not providing favours to a few, she wanted the power disconnected. Considering the fragile situation and emotions of the returnees, we could have just left them with this one light. After we turned off his only source of light, the owner threatened to throw us out. He did not speak to us again, and a week later, we moved back into our original residence, which was wonderful, like going home.

Tommy was working with Claire doing the tracing work, and Sara and Ana continued with the medical side of things. Sara was also investigating a report regarding the murder of ten elderly civilians from the village of Uzdolje. All those murdered were between sixty-two and seventy-nine years old, except for one twenty-eight-year-old man. He was said to have a certificate proving his exemption from serving in the army due to having a developmental disability. He was murdered anyway. Prosecuting these crimes would be future work for the International Criminal Court Tribunal in The Hague. Sara's work was to find out what she could and submit a report to the ICRC in Geneva.

During and after the attack, Emma had been feeding and looking after abandoned cats outside, and often inside, the delegation. One kitten, Ginger, had taken up permanent-resident status on the couch in the radio room. This cat was traumatised, and anyone who went near it, apart from Emma, was scratched.

Claire, on the other hand, had been looking after an equal, and growing, number of stray dogs. One dog refused to go outside and became a real nuisance in the delegation. One morning, as Mia and I prepared to head out on patrol, Emma asked me to relocate this dog to the countryside. With the lure of food, we got the poor dog into the back of the Cruiser and drove off. Thirty kilometres later, we arrived where we had left off our search the day before. The dog was eager to get out, and we drove off, leaving him to fend for himself. Later that afternoon, I received a radio call informing me the dog was back inside the delegation and refusing to move. It was a mystery how he had found his way back and I thought he had more than earned his place under one of our desks.

Towards the end of the day, we saw a Croatian military Jeep parked outside an undamaged house. I got out and spoke to the soldier standing there smoking a cigarette. He told us he was an American and although he had never set foot in the former Yugoslavia, his Croatian grandparents insisted he join the Croatian military as an officer and fight against the Serbs. He advised us that the random ARSK soldiers left behind were shooting at any vehicles travelling on the roads outside of Knin. With his professional demeanour and clean, pressed combat fatigues, he made a nice change from the rear-echelon occupation troops who were under very little control.

He told us an old man lived in the loft above the cowshed; he could not walk and needed help. Walking up the old stone steps, I wondered who climbed those same stairs during the previous world war. When I opened the weathered wooden door, the heat and fetid smell made me gasp. As our eyes became accustomed to the gloom, we saw the man who told us that his wife, daughter, son-in-law and three grandchildren left for Serbia on the first day of Operation Storm. They took what they could carry in the back of the trailer pulled by the ancient family tractor. Hearing this, I wondered if the old man's family had abandoned their tractor and belongings, as so many did, and headed off into the hills on foot. It was hard to imagine the fear of being caught up in the fighting, trying to get your wife, her aged mother, three children and what you could carry across thirty kilometres of the Dinaric Mountain range in the summer heat. Many did get to safety, but many also perished on the way. The subsequent tales of suffering from the displaced persons camps in Serbia made harrowing reading.

Even with the loft door wide open, the odour in the room was almost unbearable. But this old man wanted to talk. Giving him a bottle of water to drink, he said, with tears in his eyes, "I've lived through a world war, now this. I don't understand what's going on, brother fighting brother. Why?"

I had no answer for him. He had decided to stay as he didn't want to burden his family. In the panic to leave, his daughter and son-in-law carried him upstairs, left food and water, but this had quickly gone bad or run out. He was unable to get out of bed to use the latrine bucket and apologised for the mess.

He told us that he had fought as a partisan with Tito during the Second World War, was wounded twice, and saw his three brothers taken away by the Nazis, never to be seen again. He married the girl of his dreams, bought this farm, had children, then grandchildren and built a life, only to see everything lost and destroyed. I doubted he would see his family again. At seventy-nine, he was of sound mind; listening to this once-proud freedom fighter, husband, father and grandfather, I felt sad and helpless. I wished there was more I could do for him. Could I find his wife, his family, give him back some dignity? No, all I could do was listen to his life story. The half-hour we spent listening to his tale was a precious glimpse of humanity amidst a sea of inhumanity.

I radioed the delegation to let Sara and Emma know I was bringing him to the hospital. If we left him, and the ragtag army found him or just burnt the house and barn down, he would die alone. He was relieved to be going to the hospital. Carrying him down the crumbling stone stairs was easier than I thought. He was as light as a feather.

The spiffy Croatian officer said there was a body of another man two houses farther down the road. Leaving Mia chatting with our patient, I took a blanket and found the body of a man curled up in the foetal position. He looked to be about fifty and had been shot dead outside his house. Someone had already partially covered him with a bedspread. Feeling a little sick, I asked the officer to inform the sanitation squad to come to collect the body.

Sara was at the Knin hospital when we arrived; she helped us carry the stretcher up the three flights of stairs to the floor being used for the elderly. The few staff were overwhelmed and didn't really want another patient; they relented when Sara reminded them that the hospital operated only through supplies from us, the Red Cross. We left wondering, *What would happen to the old man?*

It was Mia's last day; she would now work from the Split delegation. After thanking her for her help in difficult circumstances, I saw her off in the Cruiser sent to collect her. Tomorrow, Slava, my new field officer and translator, whom I had briefly met a few times previously, would arrive from Zagreb.

Before we could stop for the day, Tommy and I took the truck to the warehouse and loaded food, water and blankets, enough for six busloads of civilians expelled from the strategically important town of Doboj, where the ARSK had committed many instances of war crimes and ethnic cleansing. During the 1992 Bosnian war, more than 5,500 shells were fired into the town, killing 100 and wounding 400 civilians. These forces were implicated in large-scale raping, torturing and killing of civilians, as well as daily looting and destruction of homes. From a pre-war population of 70,000, these few people were the last to be forcibly removed from their homes.

Three hundred and sixty women, children and elderly waited in the school gym with a few men. The school was merely a transit stop for them. Tommy met me at the school with the fifteen small loaves remaining that day in the UN camp bakery. Claire had spent the afternoon at the gym, registering peoples' names and having Red Cross Messages filled out. The refugees welcomed the food and water as they had spent the entire day travelling to Knin packed into the hot, airless, Soviet-era buses. The following day, they moved into a large, displaced persons camp in Central Bosnia to begin a life with little hope of returning to their hometown.

August 16th

The Swiss delegate working closely with the Croatian Red Cross finished off what Tommy and I started, and they worked miracles – finding tables, chairs, cutlery, crockery, even tablecloths and everything else needed to operate the public food kitchen. The doors opened that morning.

Tommy and I saw the first customers, thirty elderly people, queuing patiently for a hot meal. Among them, I saw the old lady who had sheltered with us during the first terrifying days of Operation Storm. She noticed us and was near to tears as we gave her a quick hug. Clearly, she had decided to remain in Knin.

We then headed to the warehouse to fuel up the Cruiser. The police guard we were supposed to have was nowhere to be seen, but the door swinging open told me we had been broken into again. I radioed Sara and told her she should come and see what had been taken from her dwindling medical supplies. The hidden fuel supply was still intact, so I filled jerrycans and carried them out to the Cruiser, ready for the day's work. Sara would get her supplies replaced by the next convoy from either Split or Zagreb. She would attempt to insist that General Čermak put a stop to this incessant looting of our supplies.

My bicycle, bought at the French PX in Split, was the one item I had taken with me from the residence to the delegation, early the morning of August 4th. I had unwisely moved it to the warehouse when our workspace was becoming crowded with the addition of our Split teams. I thought I had it well hidden upstairs, but alas, it was stolen, no doubt now being ridden by a blasted looter. *Maybe this was my way out of cycling home in a month or so!*

Our work continued more to the east, closer to the Dinaric Mountains. Emma had received reports over the last few days of more houses and farms being burnt and their inhabitants being beaten and harassed. With Sara, Claire and the two teams from Zagreb also out in the field with us, five vehicles covered over 10,000-square kilometres. There were still no other humanitarian NGOs operating in the area.

The Croatian authorities declared Operation Storm complete on August 8, 1995. Eight days later, as Slava and I drove from village to village, hamlet to hamlet and saw the fresh destruction and burning houses with sporadic gunfire echoing around, I wondered how complete the operation was. We saw few intact houses during our search. Many of the old folk we found in these houses were Croatian and displayed the Croatian flag. That they were not Serbian helped to protect them from the orgy of pillage and destruction, but there were no guarantees in this aftermath of war. They were as terrified as any of the other ethnic groups and needed our help equally.

An old lady – it was almost always an old lady – walked out into the road and reported that an old man had been living in his cow shed for the last two weeks. She had been trying to help but could not do any more for him. After we registered her, she walked us over to the shed. The only light was from the holes in the roof and walls. As our eyes adjusted to the darkness, we spotted him lying on some sort of bed covered with a filthy sheepskin despite the heat under the tin roof. The old lady stayed outside and held the door open to let in some light and air. The filth this poor old man had been lying in was shocking.

Slava and I quickly put on a pair of latex gloves. I took the sheepskin rug off his bed and put it on the slime on the floor, then put the stretcher on top. I took hold of his birdlike shoulders and, with Slava lifting his feet, we gently laid him on the stretcher. We told him we would take him to the hospital. After muttering a few words, he was silent as we slid the stretcher into the rear of the Cruiser. With tears in her eyes, the old lady thanked us. We negotiated potholes, rubble, broken-down tractors and cars, and the occasional dead cow. The old man did not utter a word, and I tried to keep the drive as smooth as possible.

We met Tommy and Sara at the hospital, and our passenger totally surprised us by asking Sara what part of Canada she came from - in perfect English! It never ceased to amaze me how interconnected we all were. Here was a frail and abandoned old man, picking up on Sara's Canadian accent, and inquiring about her home. Once upstairs, a nurse and Tommy started to undress him. He sat on the floor, too weak to help much but trying to keep his dignity. He held his hands around his groin but had to lift his arms when his filthy undershirt was pulled off. I was rooted to the spot, unable to help, watching clouds of dry skin fall from him like talcum powder. Dressed in a patched but clean hospital gown, he reached down and picked up a small leather pouch; he said it held all the money he had. Throughout, Tommy's usual compassion shone through.

The people we found had lost everything they ever had, except their lives. I was humbled to see their strength and dignity in the face of this calamity. I knew I would always be marked by these people and their fortitude.

CHAPTER 14

A Few Days in Paradise

• • • • •

While the others attended a meeting at the UN camp, I sat on the couch drinking a cold beer and chatting to Sara while she cooked dinner. We talked about Canada, England, the weather and what would happen after we finished our work here. We covered everything we had kept bottled up for the last few weeks. Emma had just that afternoon said Sara and I would be able to take a few days of compensation leave in Split, starting in two days. We were thrilled to be able to spend some real time together. From the Split waterfront, the beautiful islands of Brac and Hvar were just a one-hour ferry ride away. We'd be close enough if we needed to return quickly, and we could revel in peace and quiet, away from the chaos.

Tommy, with the help of our landlady, cleaned and repaired the damage caused by the Croatian soldiers during their brief stay in our main residence. Our five-man team would stay together, with Sara, Claire and I once again occupying the main floor of the house, and Emma and Tommy moving into Stanko's family's apartment upstairs. Stanko's mother remained downstairs to prevent their home from being possessed by the returning population or those coming to settle in the area. Tommy and I moved our pitiful possessions back. Looking around, I saw the scant remains of Stanko's belongings. He and his family were most likely living in a tent provided by the Red Cross or the UNHCR in a displaced persons camp somewhere in Serbia.

Tommy and I went to Emma's former apartment and found only a few pots and pans remaining. On the walk back, we stopped outside a grocery store completely destroyed by a direct hit. Sitting amongst the rubble was a small, unbroken bottle of Russian Vodka. Quick as a flash, Tommy had it in his pocket. He pretended not to hear me when I told him I would have to report his action as another incident of looting. Mysteriously, I found it empty two days later in the fridge.

We had three nervous dogs living on our balcony; I didn't know how many cats Emma had upstairs in her apartment. The shooting had died down, but now and again at night, we heard bursts of automatic gunfire echoing through the deserted streets. The noise upset the poor dogs; Claire fed them secretly because Emma forbade them on the premises. A typical evening would be the five of us arriving at our house at different times. The first ones to arrive, usually Tommy and I, would start preparing a delicious ration-pack dinner; spaghetti was a favourite.

Emma was usually the last to arrive, and we created a variety of ploys to keep her away from the balcony. If she was heading out for a cigarette, someone would head out the front door and ask her a question, thereby enticing her outside; or cut her off on her path to the balcony by telling her an event of the day, grabbing her elbow and steering her back into the kitchen. We did this out of the deep respect we had for her, and not wanting to upset the balance in the group. We didn't want to take sides over seemingly small issues, wanted to keep the peace and wanted everyone's coping mechanisms observed – in this case, stray animals.

One old dog, who had had too many puppies, took a liking to me. With her dirty orange-and-white coat showing a life of abuse and hardship, she would push her way inside from the balcony to sit as close to me as possible, trembling at the first hint of gunfire outside.

My orange-and-white training partner, 1995

Two days went by in a blur as Sara and I anticipated our coming four-day holiday. We needed to be back at the delegation by eight on Tuesday morning. The others had no idea we were spending compensation time together, nor where we were going. With one small bag each and a quick goodbye, off we went in Sara's Land Cruiser

542. We headed across the bridge, past the UN camp still teeming with displaced persons, past the long-abandoned Serb checkpoint, up the hill and out onto the flat plain that gently sloped down over the next thirty kilometres, until we reached the coast road. With the sparkling Adriatic on our right and the mountains separating us from the aftermath of war to the left, we drove on into Split and couldn't keep the smiles off our faces.

Tomislav, one of my ex-field officers, had offered his Ficu, a Yugoslav-made Fiat 500, for us to use. I got to know him very well during many arduous convoys into Central Bosnia. Tomislav was not much older than his car of twenty years. But he appeared timeworn on the rare occasions he talked about his days as a soldier in the JNA.

Once, at the very beginning of the Yugoslav wars, he and his JNA platoon were tasked with occupying a particular hill in the north, near the Slovenian border. His commanding officer said the position was safe and unlikely to be shelled. As he related this tale to me, his normally excellent English became progressively worse. After setting up their observation post, they came under such a well-orchestrated artillery barrage that it was clear they had been given the wrong information. This command was simply a trap to kill as many as possible and make it look like a wartime incident. The JNA was going through the same breakup turmoil along ethnic divides as was Yugoslavia. The majority of Tomislav's platoon was Muslim and Croatian, but most of the officer core were Serbian. He escaped back down the hill, leaving behind many dead comrades. Soon after, he published a book about his experiences, with all the proceeds going to a Croatian charity for wounded soldiers.

Seeing Tomislav again reminded me of one humorous incident on our way to Tuzla with a nine-truck convoy. At the Ribnica Shooting Gallery, everyone knew the drill and had donned their bullet-proofs. Well, honestly, I almost fell over when I looked at how Tomislav had got his head jammed into one armhole, one arm sticking out where the head hole was and the other arm hanging out where the waist should be. To top it all off, he managed to pull all the Velcro straps tight, and he seemed to be having difficulty breathing. I was also having difficulty breathing because I was laughing so much. Experienced as he was, he'd succumbed to the tense atmosphere and forgot how to put on his bullet-proof jacket.

The Ficu on Hvar, 1995

The Ficu had seen many a mile and at least two engine changes. The engine was, as the name suggests, a 500cc motor, the size of a small motorcycle engine. But, apart from a cloud of blue smoke and some gentle wheezing coming from the second-hand motor, it started and ran nicely. Looking like a couple of tourists in a stolen car, Sara and I drove onto the ferry en route to the paradise of Hvar. Standing in the sunshine at the ship's rail, we felt like the luckiest people on earth as we watched the blue Adriatic Sea tumble past, leaving a wide, frothy wake that disappeared as the boat forged ahead to Stari Grad, one of the oldest ports in Europe. Only local people were on board; the tourists who would have thronged the islands in this part of the Croatian Adriatic before the war had stayed away for four years. Previously, eighty percent of Hvar's income came from tourism, largely Europeans, and now the island's 11,000 residents were suffering. However, it certainly was the most beautiful place to sit out the war.

Once off the ferry, we drove across the island toward the main town. The road went over the spine of small mountains covered in pine forests, vineyards, olive groves and perfumed lavender fields that ran the length of the island. Halfway up, I decided to investigate why the engine was groaning. I lifted the bonnet in the rear of the car; the little motor appeared to be overheating due to its unaccustomed mountain exertion. Sara noticed a small stick tucked up near the oil filler, with the words "use this stick for longer journeys" written on it in English. With the stick holding up the bonnet, the by-now-cooler motor happily surged to the top of the mountain. Then we simply turned off the engine and coasted down to the beautiful town of Hvar, which had been a major naval base in the time of the Venetian empire.

We semi-abandoned the car outside one of the few bars still open. After sipping our first cool beer, we asked the barman if he knew of any accommodation available. "I have a cousin that has an apartment that you could rent for your stay," he offered. The cousin arrived in a flash and took us on the two-minute walk across St. Stephen Square to his one-bedroom rental with kitchenette; his rate was more than reasonable at ten DM per day. The waterfront still had a few very nice restaurants open, waiting for the war to end. We spent our days swimming in the warm sea, wining and dining, talking, making love and sleeping. The conflict on the mainland just sixty kilometres away seemed to be on the other side of the world. We were in heaven, rested and at peace.

The morning of our last day on the island, we noticed the car had been moved to another part of the car park. Inside, on the driver's seat, was a huge bag of onions. The barman, who by now knew us quite well, explained we had parked in the way of a produce delivery truck. The Ficu's unlocked doors with the key stuck in the ignition made it easy to move; the onions were a "sorry about moving your car" gift from the delivery driver. A nice surprise. After struggling up the mountain with the long-journey stick in place and rolling down the other side with the engine turned off, Tomislav's trusty little car triumphantly scraped its underside on the ferry loading ramp and wheezed to a stop.

Tomislav was happy to see his beloved car back and still running strong. I offered him a carton of Marlboro smokes as a token of our gratitude, but being the gentleman he was, he refused them. He was happy with the onions.

Our plan was to spend the last night in the lovely old port town of Šibenik, thirty kilometres north of Split. Off we drove in our Land Cruiser; washed, serviced and fuelled by the excellent ICRC workshop staff. Before heading to Šibenik, I decided to call into the British UN contingent, the 1st Battalion, the Cheshire Regiment headquarters, a couple of kilometres south, to see if I could buy a bicycle at the PX to replace the one stolen from the Knin warehouse. Over the previous four days, Sara had convinced me to re-animate my planned bicycle trek home to England. I spied an aluminium-framed mountain bike, which I knew could do the journey. Clearly, I was now committed to cycling home at the end of my mission.

CHAPTER 15

Farewell

* * * * *

"Knin, Knin. This is mobile 542, mobile 542. Do you copy, over?"

"This is Knin. Go ahead 542."

"Mobile 542 entering Knin. Next contact delegation in fifteen minutes."

"Well copied. See you soon."

The few buildings on the main street that were still smouldering when we left had burnt out. Remaining were the familiar piles of rubble including charred timbers mixed with pots and pans, the twisted remains of an iron bed frame, a fridge and a stove, all blackened and ruined.

Everyone was pleased to see us back. We were introduced to the fresh teams, recently arrived from Zagreb. The food assessment in the surrounding areas had been completed, and we now had a logistics delegate to take care of the distribution and supply. I was very happy to see Chris had been posted to Knin for this work.

Sara went straight back to work that morning at her desk in the now-tidy delegation offices. Now that we had so much more help from the Zagreb teams, Tommy and I had less to do. The power had been restored to most of the town, along with running water. Judging by the even larger piles of rubbish in the streets, it looked like double the number of new settlers had arrived to stake their claim.

I found a small military knapsack among the rubbish piles which would be handy for my bike ride home across Europe. Due to the interventions made by Emma and Sara with General Čermak, the arbitrary murders, burnings and looting in the town and country-side had all but ceased. The extra presence from the Zagreb teams also had an impact. Tommy and I worked at the warehouse to get it cleaned up and organized for an arriving aid convoy and we had three daily workers/settlers helping us.

I had just a few weeks left to complete my fourth mission in the former Yugoslavia. If the cycle home was going to happen, I needed to get fit. Tommy said he could take care of the rest of the work and urged me to go for a bike ride. Perfect – the weather was nice and warm. With a VHF in my backpack just in case, and my skeletal orange-and-white dog trotting alongside, off I went.

It seemed my little canine companion was more out of shape than I was. After valiantly trying to keep up with my slow walk up to the top of the hill out of town, she was so out of breath and quiver-ing I decided to sit her in the shade. I'd return in half an hour, and we'd go back down together. It is common knowledge that dogs are unable to cry, but I was sure she was on the verge of tears, thinking I was going to abandon her at the top of the hill. I rode on for a little more, past abandoned goods and vehicles serving as mute testament to the people who fled for their lives.

There was not a sound, just the murmur of the gentle wind and the birds singing. I turned around by an abandoned Zastava twenty-millimetre triple-barrelled anti-aircraft gun. Although these weapons were commonplace, I was surprised to see it was still there. Because of the high cost, armies normally retrieve heavy weaponry from the battlefield as soon as possible. Suddenly, there was an almighty explosion in the field just across the road. I was stunned by the power and violence of the blast. When my ears stopped ringing, all I could hear was the wind still blowing through the trees. The birds had decided to go elsewhere and sing.

Destroyed ARSK tank – post-Oluja, 1995

The dog was happy that I really did return for her. I explained the explosion was probably a mine triggered by a cow and gave her a belly rub. We set off walking back down the hill as she was still too tired to go any faster. This was to be my training regime for the next two weeks. Walk up the hill, leave orange-and-white companion in the shade to catch her breath, go for a real ride for about half an hour, collect my still-exhausted dog, and walk back down the hill. On a few occasions I tried to sneak past our balcony where the dogs lived, only to find the orange-and-white one glued to my rear wheel. I got to like that dog.

We were having distinguished guests for dinner. Emma had been visited by two Croatian Army colonels earlier that afternoon who would, "Come and cook dinner at your place to get to know you and the ICRC better." At six thirty they knocked, and Claire let in the two big guys. One said to the other, "Oops, Red Cross building. We must take off our sidearms." They each made a show of hiding their pistols under the couch cushions.

Glancing around at our bemused looks, Sara offered them a glass of wine. Nine months ago, one of them was a café bar owner and the other worked in a print shop in Split. And they came across this way, as civilians dressed as soldiers. After several glasses of wine and a long explanation from the guy at the stove cooking a large pot of mussels on how great the Croatian military machine was and what a spectacular victory Operation Storm was, somehow forgetting to mention the civilian atrocities that were still happening, we sat down and started eating.

Mussels are the last thing I would order from a menu. The others enjoyed their large plates. Not me. I sat next to Sara, trying to hold a conversation with the two guests and desperately trying to figure out how to reduce the load of wobbly pink objects on my plate. The second I thought no one was looking, I attempted to throw a handful onto Sara's plate, but my aim was thrown off by her foot caressing my leg under the table. A large handful of hot mussels skidded across the plastic tablecloth to land with a clatter on the floor. Maybe the two imposters in slightly stained combat fatigues did have a semblance of manners. They ignored the clatter and continued as if nothing had happened.

Two hours later, once all the wine in the house had been consumed by our guests, they retrieved their pistols and with a cheery
adieu, off they went in their Soviet military Jeep, followed by a cloud
of blue smoke.

After our guests departed, Sara told us that one of our housekeep-
ers, a local Serbian woman, had been raped in Knin on her way
home the previous night. She came into the delegation that morning
and told Sara what had happened. Sara had been at the Croatian
military headquarters all day, trying to get something done about
this and the many other rapes reported, committed by the Croatian
occupation soldiers. The fight to get justice for our housekeeper was
almost impossible, but Sara, determined, had harangued General
Čermak all day. She told us how frustrating it was being blocked
at every turn. The end of this sad tale was that a month or so later,
Sara twice accompanied the housekeeper to see a judge in the coastal
town of Zadar. He listened to our housekeeper's story, questioned
her, and determined that it was her fault, if indeed she was raped,
for not fighting off her attacker. Sadly, not an uncommon verdict for
reported rapes worldwide – blaming the victim.

As if that had not been enough for one evening, Tommy confessed
that he had crashed the MAN at the same bridge where the Nigerian
UN troops had gone over the side. As he was crossing, he was obliged
to avoid a large oncoming APC and ended upside down at the foot
of the bridge, luckily unharmed. The UN crew quickly arrived and
recovered the truck, leaving it outside our warehouse. We would go
there first thing in the morning to see if it was worth sending to the
Split workshops for repair.

The displaced persons at the UN camp were to be transported to
Serbia in bus convoys. At five on the designated morning, we stood
on our balcony and watched the sombre parade of the first exodus
of buses drive past our house and climb the hill out of Knin. They

took the same route I took to Zrmania with my cargo of terrified townsfolk, those first hours after the beginning of Operation Storm.

Another hot and sunny day. Sara was already at the delegation, and the tracing teams were out in the field. Tommy and I went to the UN camp and collected as many of our tents as we could and brought them back to the warehouse. They were no longer needed.

The tanks were now gone from the camp's main gate; the Nigerian UN soldier manning the gate motioned for us to pull over to allow more buses out of the camp to start the day's journey across the border into Serbia. I counted nine buses crammed full of people with their meagre belongings strapped on the roof or gathered in their laps. The children gazing through the dirty windows looked happy, as if they were going on a holiday to the beach. The gaunt faces of the adults told another story.

We rolled up and packed away as many still serviceable tents as we could fit into the back of the Land Cruiser and headed to our warehouse. When I saw how badly the MAN was damaged, I knew there was no hope of getting it back on the road. What did bother me was the Croatian police busily stripping anything of value from it. These police had been stationed as guards to stop any looting, and there they were, doing just that: looting. Our local warehouse staff were simply standing by and watching it happen. I parked the Cruiser right in front of the two police vans, blocking their way. Jumping out, I confronted the policeman carrying one of the truck's two large batteries. He looked me up and down with a sneer and continued to put the battery in the rear of his van, and then started to remove the other one. One of our local workers came over. "Don't cross that guy. He's special forces." Well, with these past weeks of witnessing the looting, this incident was just one theft too many for me to ignore.

First, I asked Tommy to take note of the police vehicle registration; next, I went and grabbed my truck battery out of the police van and threw it on top of the tents in the Cruiser. This caught the slightly chubby special forces guy's attention. I told him I would report him to General Čermak if he continued stealing Red Cross equipment, with the distinct possibility that he would lose his job. He thought about it, then he and the other two policemen said I should move my vehicle so they could leave.

As soon as the police left, Tommy, I and a couple of the daily workers removed anything else of value from the MAN and locked it up inside the warehouse. I suspected we hadn't seen the last of our police friends. The water tanker was still at the now-empty school, so we drove over, and I returned with the Volvo to park it at the warehouse.

Emma said she would take up the incident with General Čermak but given the results of Sara's search for justice for our housekeeper, she doubted we would get any results. I left Tommy at the house preparing dinner, got my bike out of my room and snuck down the stairs to get an hour of training in before it was too late to be out. The VHF radio was chattering gently in my backpack.

I was just starting to climb the hill when my erstwhile Tour de France training companion trotted up with her tongue hanging out; she gave me her "why did you try and sneak off?" look in between laboured breaths. Again, I made her sit in the lengthening shadows at the top of the hill to await my return. After a good hour of hard riding, I noticed my fitness level was slightly improved. Maybe, just maybe, I could complete the ride back home. In truth, there was never any maybe. I was going to cycle back to England, even if I had to walk most of the way. "Look in the dictionary," Sara said, "and under the word 'determined', there is a photo of young Roger."

My orange-and-white friend was sleeping when I returned. After a stretch, yawn, belly rub, and a good scratch, she was fully awake, and we walked back down the hill just in time for an extremely tasty dinner of chicken pasta prepared by Chef Tommy. On the balcony, the dogs secretly shared a couple of tins of dog food. That night,

I dropped off to sleep to the sound of crickets in the garden and nothing else – except maybe a solitary car going by, driven in a normal, civilized manner. After the noise and mayhem of the past weeks, the peace and quiet were a little unsettling.

The next morning, I woke up late. Everyone had left for another busy day at the delegation. As I sipped a cup of bitter coffee and listened to the traffic going past the window, a feeling of sadness swamped me. All the action, danger, fear and pure adrenaline-fuelled excitement had come to an end for me. *Why didn't I get up early with the others?* I guessed it was because I didn't need to. Maybe they also knew this and let me lie in bed a bit longer.

The staff from Zagreb were taking on all the fieldwork; Sara, Emma and Claire were as busy as ever. The public kitchen we had started a few short weeks ago was being run by the Croatian Red Cross and fed 120 people a day. We were really pleased with its success. Although looting continued, the Croatian military authorities and police were at last taking steps to try and stop it. And thanks to Sara's untiring efforts, the Knin hospital was well stocked and had enough staff to again function as it should. We had also determined there was a need for an old people's home for the remaining frail elderly and were successful in having one established at the hospital, run by the Croatian Red Cross.

I had been in contact with the BRC overseas department officer. Once I left the former Yugoslavia to head home, the ICRC would no longer be responsible for me. The officer wanted to know when I would like to fly home and where to – Gatwick or Heathrow. When I said that I was going to cycle home, she was rather surprised. I tried to explain how I had talked myself into the idea and now didn't want to disappoint those who had given me encouragement. Most of all, I was not going to let myself down.

I had sent my bike up to Zagreb with one of the tracing teams; they left it at the warehouse for me to collect later. My bike was made by Peugeot; its aluminium frame and wheels kept the weight down. The rear rack was just big enough to hold a small bag where I carried the bare minimum for three weeks on the road: one change of clothes, a toothbrush, a razor, twenty-two teabags (no clue why I had twenty-two – probably one for each day plus a spare), one large black bin bag and a Soviet military rubber, full-length raincoat I had found amongst all the rubbish piled up on the streets of Knin. Oh, and yes, the small JNA backpack where I carried my passport and some cash.

I said goodbye to Emma, Claire and Tommy with the usual promises to keep in touch. I really wasn't paying much attention because Sara and I wanted to get on the road and have our last few hours together. The others still had not twigged to our relationship, and we kept our affection in check so as not to disrupt the team dynamic. We all worked so well together, liked and deeply respected each other; we did not want to upset the balance. Sara and I planned to meet in London when she was on her way back to Canada in December.

The local Split delegation staff I had known and worked with for fifteen months had arranged a farewell dinner that night at the restaurant Kod Joze in the old town. Sara was hoping to have one last night with me and come to the dinner, but she was radioed to return to Knin before dark. Seeing her Land Cruiser drive off, blend in with the other traffic and disappear, I felt for the first time a bit lost and unsure of the future.

Everyone from the delegation came to the dinner. The excellent company and laughter were something I would never forget. They were all solid, dedicated people. A friend drove me to the airport the next morning for the last time. He handed me the ticket, shook my hand, wished me bon voyage and was gone. We had said our real goodbyes the night before in a haze of cigarette smoke and copious amounts of wine.

September 16th

Walking off the plane at Zagreb Airport, the first thing I noticed was the weather. Although still sunny, it was definitely cooler. The next morning, when I would start this much-talked-about bike ride, *Would there be snow over the Alps?*

Apart from the rubber raincoat, I was not exactly ready for cold or wet weather. My runners were a pair an Irish driver had discarded (thank you, Vincent), and they were in better condition than mine. My jacket came from the remains of a bag of donated clothing my eldest sister sent from England; it fitted rather nicely, apart from the torn lining and broken zipper. Gloves I didn't have. (In truth, I am never prepared for inclement weather.) The only good thing I had was Sara's Gore-Tex rain jacket that she insisted I borrow till we met in London.

Luckily for me, the delegation had sent a driver to take me to my final night's accommodation at the Pilots' House near the airport. Thoughtfully, the warehouse manager had delivered my bike to the guest house.

★ ★ ★

From the Zagreb Airport, the ICRC operated a Lear jet flown by two British pilots, and a massive Ukrainian Ilyushin Il-76 ex-Soviet bomber flown by a crew of five Ukrainians. The Ilyushin had a payload of fifty-two tonnes and was rugged enough to be able to land on unpaved runways. The cargo compartment was twenty metres long by three and a half metres wide by three and a half metres tall and was designed to be ramp-loaded and carry oversize loads.

The previous summer, I had been tasked with arranging for the delivery of three very large emergency generators to Sarajevo. The sorely needed generators had sat on the Split airport tarmac for three months, awaiting clearance from the Serbian authorities. Due to intense international pressure, permission had at last been granted.

With the Split ICRC relief delegate, I supervised the loading. The Ukrainian loadmaster soon had them fitted into the plane's fuselage and strapped down, ready for the one-hour flight to Sarajevo. I thought my part of this delivery was complete until the relief delegate asked me if I wanted to accompany the generators to Sarajevo and supervise the unloading. The only time I had been to Sarajevo was ten years previously, on my way back from Baghdad to pick up a load of children's bicycles for delivery to England, at a time when Yugoslavia was prosperous and peaceful. Not wanting to miss a chance to see Sarajevo again, I ran up the ramp and excitedly made my way past the load and into the cavernous cockpit. The flight crew were already strapped into their seats, with the navigator in the lower bomb-aimers pod. Shouting over the roar of the Soloviev turbofan engines, I asked where my seat was. The pilot didn't seem at all concerned to see a non-manifested person suddenly appear in the cockpit and was as equally unconcerned when he pointed to a suitcase at the back of the co-pilots' seat for me to sit on. By this time, we were thundering down the rapidly shortening runway. My death grip on the back of the seat and the grip I was exerting on my sphincter eased at the same time as the aircraft lifted off, clearing the airport perimeter fence by millimetres.

Watching the pilot, co-pilot and engineer handle the beast; I was struck by how similar it was to driving a large, heavy truck (without the "you could die in seconds" part). With a couple of empty Coke cans, some orange peel and discarded cigarette packets sloshing around in what appeared to be a water-filled trough in the lower floor section, we miraculously achieved cruising altitude. Everyone lit cigarettes. The two pilots seemed to know what they were doing, so at 20,000 feet over Bosnia, after my fourth delicious cigarette, I stopped shaking and adopted an air of relaxed coolness. Everyone's eyes smarted from the suffocating cloud of smoke obscuring the view out the window. One hour later, cigarettes were extinguished, tray tables stowed and seats put in the upright position, just in time for the most fun part of the flight.

I knew we were going to die when I saw the two Coke cans and the empty smoke packets, along with a small piece of mummified salami that I hadn't noticed earlier, suddenly become weightless as the flying truck began the landing approach – and I use the term loosely. This consisted of flying along fairly level up in the blue sky only to drop like a seventy-tonne stone vertically, heading for a fiery crash onto the shell-pocked runway. At the very last moment, with arm and leg sinews straining, the two flying truck drivers brought the shuddering aircraft under control and touched down as light as a feather.

The five minutes it took to taxi to a deserted part of the airport, past the wreck of a Belgian Ilyushin shot down just a few months before while attempting to land in the normal way, was just enough time for me to bring my emotions under control and stop myself from weeping with relief.

I later learned this was the standard for landing at the Sarajevo airport during the war; it was called the "Khe Sanh Approach", developed by the US Air Force during the Vietnam War. At four thousand feet, the aircraft dives steeply and, at the last minute, levels off and quickly puts down, giving the attacking Serbian forces much less time to get to their guns and start shooting. A normal level approach left the aircraft exposed to small-arms and rocket fire for too long. The novel method demanded nerves of steel and skilled aircraft handling.

The siege of Sarajevo was the longest of any capital city in the history of modern warfare. Serb forces along with the JNA, besieged Sarajevo from April 5, 1992, until February 29, 1996. Surrounding the city under the command of General Ratko Mladic, a small force of 18,000 well-equipped Serbs continually assaulted the largely defenceless city (approximately 526,000 civilians) with mortars, tank rounds, heavy artillery, rocket launchers, aircraft-launched rocket bombs and sniper fire. Killed were 11,541 including 1,500 children; additionally, the 56,000 wounded included 15,000 children. The 70,000 poorly equipped ARBiH Bosnian government defence forces inside the city were unable to break the siege.

As soon as the plane shuddered to a halt with the engines still running and the ramp down, the Ukrainian load master and a large armoured French UN forklift started to unload the cargo. Edging our way past the generators, I and the four-flight crew jumped down onto the tarmac. Looking closely, I noted that the forklift driver was wearing his Kevlar helmet and a bulletproof jacket. A few seconds later, a French UN armoured Land Rover skidded to a halt, and the driver shouted for me and the Ukrainians to move around to the other side of the aircraft, out of the view of the snipers who were always on the lookout for targets. A short thirty minutes later, we were unloaded.

Their next stop was Zagreb, but I really had to return to Split. About 200-metres across the tarmac was an ICRC Learjet hurriedly loading three ICRC personnel, all dressed in flak jackets and helmets. As I hoped, the plane was heading to Split. But the pilot said there was no way he could take me; I wasn't on their manifest. "You will have to fly out the way you came in." I had no idea I was such an Olympian-class runner until two mortar rounds fired from the surrounding hills landed on the edge of the runway and exploded in two simultaneous columns of black soil.

Breathlessly, I reclaimed my suitcase seat, ready for take-off. The guys were happy to see me again. As they swung the aircraft around and began roaring down the well-patched runway, they motioned for me to take my suitcase seat and sit in the bomb bay for its great view.

The take-off seemed to be the reverse of Khe Sanh – really quite thrilling. I marvelled at the power and strength of this obsolete aircraft – and the stoic Ukrainians flying it. We flew west, then north, following the Adriatic coast. At 10,000 feet, my view was just spectacular; I saw the islands of Hvar, Brac and Kortula, and told myself that one day I would visit them.

The approach and landing at the Zagreb Airport were smooth and non-terrifying. With the engines shut down, the crew grabbed their suitcases, including my seat, and climbed into the waiting ICRC Cruiser. The local driver was surprised to see me. "What are you doing here? You are not on the manifest."

I had left Split that morning, planning to be back that afternoon. "At the security gate, just show the guard your ICRC pass," the driver said. "They should let you through." This probably would have worked – if my pass had not been sitting on my bedside table in Split. With the Ukrainians' bags and cases and a couple of blankets covering me on the floor, we breezed through security and arrived at the Zagreb delegation. When I asked the Welcome Desk if they could put me up for the night, their first response was, "What are you doing here? You're not on the manifest!"

★ ★ ★

When I knocked on the front door of the Pilots' House with my backpack and bag containing my wholly inadequate cycling clothing, I was welcomed in by a truck driver who had recently arrived from England along with two other English guys. They were expecting me, and over pizza and a couple of beers, grilled me about my experiences over the previous nineteen months.

"Why are you cycling home?"

I tried to explain how things were, and the effect the postings had on me. I soon gave up when I realized I could not adequately tell them everything I had witnessed, the work I had been involved in, what had happened and how I had changed. I left them and went to make sure my bike was ready for the morning. There was not much to do except check that the tires were well inflated, and my bag was secured to the rear carrier with the two bungees I had found in the Knin delegation radio room. *Had that been yesterday?* My mind was focused on my coming road trip; Knin was consigned to the past for now. I'd have plenty of time on my ride to process all that had happened.

CHAPTER 16

The Ride

* * * * *

September 17, 1995

Falling asleep was difficult: my thoughts were everywhere, unfocused and confused. The next thing I knew, the sun was shining through the thin curtains, and the roar of the UN and civilian aircraft going about their business reminded me of where I was. The others had left the guesthouse for work earlier, except one driver who offered to give me a lift out of the city and see me on my way. I happily accepted; half an hour later, he dropped me off just outside Zagreb city limits. With his quick bon voyage, I pushed off and tried to get into a steady rhythm.

There was a chill in the air, *maybe I should have tried to find a pair of gloves*. After four hours of steady riding, I arrived at the Croatian-Slovenian border. I wondered whether to offer the Croatian border guard my ICRC ID or my passport. He took one look at the bike and waved me through, as did the Slovenian guard. I don't know what I would have replied if questions were asked about the Serbian Army backpack and the monstrously heavy rubber raincoat. Its weight was like having a small person sitting on the rear rack.

Surely it won't rain much, and how will I pedal the bike wrapped in twelve kilos of sweaty rubber anyway? Honestly, if it were stretched out around a frame, glued and nailed, the raincoat would make quite a fine cargo-carrying canoe.

Judging by the clicking and throbbing in both my knees, my Orange-Dog-Training regime hadn't contributed to my fitness level as much as I had hoped. I wondered what she was doing at that moment. *Sleeping in the shade? Awaiting my return?* I left the raincoat-canoe at the next bus stop; I hoped its next finder would have more fun with it than I did.

Next stop: Ljubljana. I didn't have a map, but no fear: my confidence was at an all-time high; I was convinced the route I was taking would end there.

The road went up and down, but mostly up, with me mainly walking and hobbling. After four hours, I began to have doubts about my unerring sense of direction. The traffic had petered out, leaving me alone, confidence shaken. After one more hour, near the snow-covered summit of a lonely Slovenian mountain, with darkness and the temperature falling fast, my first reaction was panic. The black bin bag would be no protection against the minus twenty degree Celsius wind-chill during the night. When the mountain rescue people found my body, they would probably say, "He would have survived if only he had picked up that twelve-kilo Serbian Army rubber raincoat!"

With no bicycle light, inadequately clothed, and still pedalling/walking up the mountain, I decided to just keep going, all night if necessary. I wished I were back in Knin, in the cosy bomb shelter.

My motto, *There must be a harder way*, came to mind. It was dark when I glimpsed the warm glow of lights; getting closer, I saw a genuine Alpine chalet ski resort. The lobby was empty and stone cold, but still warmer than outside, with the bonus of being safe from wolves and bears.

Eventually, a young guy spotted me and was surprised when I asked for a room. "The ski season is still three weeks away," he said. After discussing the matter at length, he took pity on me and showed me to a small room that was equally as cold as the lobby. After warming my freezing body with the small hair drier anchored to the bathroom wall by a stout chain, I fell into a solid dreamless sleep. In the morning, after paying for the room and without breakfast, I retraced my route back down the mountain. Despite the cold and regretting not having gloves, I thoroughly enjoyed the high-speed, two-hour descent.

Back down in the lovely Slovenian lowlands, I stopped at the first gas station and bought a map of Europe and a pair of inexpensive gloves, the type made from recycled plastic bottles. I had to admit having warm hands was quite pleasant.

My plan was to keep moving all day, except during the few minutes I allowed myself to stop and buy a sandwich and a bottle of water. I would continue while I consumed my lunch in between laboured breaths. When the gradient got just too steep to carry on pedalling, I made sure the wheels did not stop turning as I jumped off the bike and continued on foot. I felt it was very important to keep the wheels in motion.

By this time, I'd had enough of cycling uphill, but the ride down was thrilling. Only once did I very nearly lose control of the bike on a rare straight section heading down a mountain into Austria. The small computer on my handlebars showed my speed at sixty-five kilometres an hour. My hands were stiff and slightly frozen (note: inexpensive gloves). By the time I managed to get some strength

into them to start applying pressure on the flimsy front and rear
brake levers, the straight piece of road had turned into a typical
Alpine Mountain hairpin. The low, beautifully built stone wall was
just high enough to stop a bicycle in the event of a collision, but
cleverly designed to catapult the unfortunate rider clear of the trees
and into space, to land somewhere below the clouds onto the mist-
shrouded valley floor 1,000 metres below. I did briefly wonder if my
mummified remains would ever be discovered. Happily, my fantas-
tic bike-handling skills saved the day! I performed the remainder
of my downhill riding in a more controlled manner. Anyway, my
body would most likely have been eaten by wild animals long before
mummification took hold.

Germany, on the ride home, 1995

The Alps cross eight countries for over 1,200 kilometres. Mont Blanc is the highest mountain in the range, rising to 4,800 metres on the Italian-French border. Compared to the Himalayas, these mountains are small. But after I cycled and walked up and over them, again and again for eight days, I can testify they were anything but small. From the Slovenian Alps over to the Italian Alps. Through Italy, then across the Austrian Alps, through Austria, then over the German Alpine range and down into the relatively flat plains of Germany, France and Belgium.

My average speed in the mountains was thirteen kilometres per hour; on less hilly roads, my average was seventeen. I have always weighed sixty-eight kilograms give or take, and after working in the difficult conditions in the former Yugoslavia, I had no spare fat. I expended so much energy on the bike that I got skinnier by the day – even though I ate like a horse every night.

Each afternoon, near four o'clock, I would start looking for somewhere to stay for the night. Accommodation was not easy to find on a bicycle. Forty kilometres to the next village was not far in a vehicle, but was considerably longer on a bike, with still no guarantee of accommodation. I was getting fitter and would have loved to ride later into the day, but I decided not to risk having to sleep out, wrapped in my thin black bin bag in a damp field.

At this stage, I had evenly distributed across Europe my few surplus items not needed for basic survival. I was down to one change of underwear and one pair of socks. Even the remaining teabags had been jettisoned. When it wasn't raining there was a good strong headwind, but it seemed every other day I had the pleasure of both rain and wind.

Some hotels were happy to see me, and some, taking one look at my damp clothing and wild unkempt appearance, pretended they had no spare rooms. In the twenty-one days it took to get home, I stayed in a dozen very expensive hotels.

One upscale hotel accepted my plea for one night's accommodation. The uniformed porter, quickly realizing there was no chance of any type of gratuity being slipped into his hand, flung open the door to my room and almost pushed me in. Turning quickly on his heels, he hurried to show other, wealthier guests to their rooms, no doubt hoping for a large denomination note.

After a long hot shower before dinner, I arranged my damp socks and underwear on a short length of string across the bath. I fixed the hotel hairdryer switch in the ON position with an elastic band and cunningly positioned a stream of warm air over my laundry. Dinner was a pleasant, though quiet affair. I had been seated near the large double kitchen doors by the same guy who showed me to my room; the well-heeled guests had no opportunity to engage with me in conversation or light-hearted banter. I was able to eat quite fast as, even though the food was well-cooked and piping hot, the draught from the constantly swinging door handily cooled my dinner.

Two hours later, I was savouring a small cigar – yes, this place was so classy that smoking at the table was not only permitted, it was positively encouraged. My second glass of expensive cognac slowly soaked through the large piece of black forest gateau. That, in turn, was sitting heavily on top of the chicken cordon bleu, sloshing around with the excellent soup and fresh buttered rolls in my alarmingly distended stomach. Only my iron will prevented me from vomiting it all back up.

Back in my room, I noticed a funny smell – the same smell one gets when electrical wires are burning. The 120 minutes it took for me to eat my delicious dinner was 115 minutes too long for the small hotel hairdryer to run. Another five minutes and the hotel would have been fully ablaze, sadly reducing my underwear and socks to ashes.

All day, every day, as I pedalled my bike slowly northwards and home, my recent experiences ran through my mind like an endless film. I was trying to put things into perspective, but not having much success. Not once did I stop to rest or do any sightseeing. My focus was totally on the ride; every turn of the wheels brought me closer to the end.

On one of the two sunny days of the entire trip, I found myself pedalling along a quiet country road in northern France, not far from the city of Arras in the department Pas-de-Calais. Arras had almost been destroyed during the First World War but was rebuilt at great cost to the French taxpayers. Thinking about the millions of soldiers and civilians killed and wounded during the war on the very land I slowly travelled over, I also recalled my grandfather, Private Thomas Fowler, wounded and spending three years as a prisoner of war. He died soon after his release at the end of the war in 1918. I have amongst his medals a letter handwritten by King George VI welcoming him home.

I will always wonder what came over me that day, with the sun casting long shadows over the gently rolling chalk plain. I saw neither car nor person and heard only the swish of my tires on the road, the distant cry of the common swift hunting for insects high above and the murmur of the early October breeze. For the first time in a long time, my mind was completely clear and untroubled. A profound and tranquil feeling flooded my senses. Minutes later, it was gone, leaving me feeling restful and at peace. I have never before or since experienced anything like it. Afterwards, my thoughts returned to the millions of lost souls perhaps still wandering those French fields. *Was it my moment of grace? Who knows for sure?*

At the end of one particularly hard day, after 146 wet and windy kilometres, I found a small pension just over the French side of the German-French border. If there had been any tourist trade at all in this small, drab and gritty industrial town, there was certainly none that afternoon. The pension bore the grand title of *Le Chef du Rhône*.

There was no menu available, there didn't appear to be a chef, and we were many miles from *le Rhône*.

The day's slog on the bike had robbed me of the little French I knew. I did manage to ask for a glass of beer which loosened my tongue enough to ask for something with, "Lots of potatoes and onion, *s'il vous plait*." Waiting for dinner to arrive, I wrote a long letter to Sara, as I did every evening. The accumulated rain slowly dripped off my clothing, through my runners and seeped through the gaps in the worn wooden floorboards. The second glass of beer lifted my spirits considerably; feeling a little light-headed, I tucked into my plate of steaming hot potatoes and onion.

The only other patron was a small old man sitting in the corner with his glass of pastis, quietly watching me from under his black beret. I wondered if he was a spy. Looking around, I noticed a faded photo of Charles de Gaulle as he marched down the Champs-Élysées after the liberation of Paris on August 25, 1944. On the wall opposite was a grand painting of Napoleon Bonaparte, sitting astride his white warhorse, scarlet cape blowing in the wind, sword in hand, pointing towards his next spectacular conquest on the way into Russia (and we all know how that ended).

Just as I reached out to tap on the glass partition separating the dining room and bar from the kitchen to alert the landlady and ask where my room might be, I was sure I saw the old man reach into his pocket and gently slip off the safety catch of the revolver hidden in his jacket pocket. She suddenly appeared and asked for a fairly large sum of French francs in advance payment for the room. I was so tired by this time I would have paid twice what she asked.

At any minute, I expected an old Citroën car to screech to a halt outside, and three black-leather-coated, well-groomed senior Gestapo pile out, crash through the front door and arrest me in front of the smirking landlady. I knew there would be no escape out the rear door as the Gestapo always posted a guy out back, hiding in the shadows with just the silhouette of his nose and chin showing under the jauntily angled brim of his hat. After I had endured weeks of brutal interrogation in the Nazi Paris headquarters, the outside wall would be dynamited by the brave men and women of the French Resistance. In the confusion, I would make my escape, eventually finding my way to England, where I would receive a summons to see the Queen at Buckingham Palace to receive a large gold medal for valour.

Clearly, time for bed.

We walked in silence down the cold corridor to what I hoped was my room. In the almost complete darkness, my host opened a door at the end of the corridor and scurried back to the comparative warmth of her kitchen. In the dull yellow glow from the tiny light hanging from the cracked and peeling ceiling, the bed looked interesting; its centre drooped centimetres lower than its less used outside edges. Finding no hot water and no heat further strengthened my paranoia about being in a Second World War time warp. I was still damp and needed to dry out my clothes. The only source of warmth in the room was the one fly-blown forty-watt bulb hanging from the ceiling. The one sock I managed to partially wrap around it did double duty as a shade. I arranged my other clothes on top of the covers; perhaps my emaciated body, fuelled by potatoes, onions and beer, would produce enough heat to remove some of the dampness. Lying in the lower section of the bed under my carefully arranged clothing, the outer edges of the musty mattress sprung up automatically around me. I was soon sound asleep, lulled by the sultry voice of Marlene Dietrich.

On day eighteen, I arrived at the port of Calais and hopped on the small bus designed to carry cyclists and their bikes through the Channel Tunnel (Chunnel). Any vehicles wanting to use the Chunnel, including large trucks, must drive onto a train. The doors closed and thirty-five minutes later opened in Folkstone, and off I went. The British Customs are on the French side, so all formalities are completed in Calais. A very efficient way to cross the English Channel, but the traditional cross-channel ferries offer a more civilized, though slower, way to cross; you know you are home when you see the White Cliffs of Dover appear through the sea mist.

I had arranged to meet Mum, Dad and my youngest son Alan at the Folkstone terminal. Jonathan, my eldest son, not being an avid cyclist, wisely decided to meet us at home. Alan would ride with me for the last leg of my trip.

The van driver soon had my trusty steed unloaded; I rode through the barrier to see Alan standing alongside his bike, with Mum and Dad waiting by his side. I was still in focus mode and didn't want to stop long, so after a quick hello, away we went.

One of Alan's hobbies was cycle racing against the clock over sixteen, twenty-five, and forty-kilometre distances, so he was very fit. Alan did not complain about the gruelling regime, nor did he slack off one bit. If the roles had been reversed, I think I would have whinged constantly. Three days later, with Alan still gamely following my rear wheel, we arrived at my parents' house in Swindon. I couldn't have finished the ride with a better partner.

Twenty months in the middle of someone else's conflict: 114 convoys; lots of scary moments; one field hospital in a repurposed chicken farm; one public kitchen; one bomb shelter; one field medic course and one IED course; one truckload of civilians evacuated; four days in paradise; one little white coffin; one flying visit to Sarajevo; five moves; one re-stolen truck; two vehicle thefts at gunpoint; several medical evacuations; one smuggled refugee and one smuggled radio operator; one successful Srebrenica enclave visit and several attempted Gorazde enclave visits; one prisoner-of-war camp visit; many arriving and departing delegates; several visits to the janitor's closet; one bicycle stolen; hundreds of frontline crossings; lots of snow, dust and mud; lots of small-arms, RPG and shell fire; innumerable UN security briefings; one thread-bare orange-and-white training partner; many friendships; countless swims in the Adriatic; one old folks home established; a 1,900-kilometre bike ride; and one love affair later, I was back home in Swindon.

Mum, Dad and my three sisters waited in the front room, ready with a much-anticipated cup of tea for Alan and me. All the events were whirring through my head as I tried to answer their questions. I really thought I had everything put away, sorted, listed, labelled, organized and reorganized in my mind during the bike ride. But after the first few questions, my recollections were back in a muddle. I was very happy to have finished the bike trip and was looking forward to sleeping in my own bed again.

First thing the next morning, I called the Knin delegation and caught Sara just before she left to visit clinics. It was wonderful to catch up and hear all about what had been happening since I had been gone. The ICRC were still busy working in the aftermath of Operation Storm. I next called the BRC, who sounded pleased and more than a little relieved that I made it back unscathed.

"Take a couple of days to rest and then come to the offices for your debriefing and medical."

The next two days passed in a blur of sleeping, eating, sleeping, then eating again.

On the trip to London, I slept and only woke when the train or the tube slowed down for the next station. The short debriefing ended with a heartfelt thank you for all my efforts on my mission. A quick taxi ride took me to my medical appointment, which was thorough and detailed. One hour later, with a clean bill of health, I fell asleep on the train back to Swindon.

CHAPTER 17

Two Bicycles and A Snowsuit

* * * * *

Three Weeks Later

I received a call from the BRC, asking if I would be interested in driving a Land Rover to Zagreb.

"Of course, I would!"

I called Sara to let her know I would come down for a visit once I had delivered the vehicle. She called back a day or so later to let me know that she had discovered a family living in the most destitute of conditions. A nine-month-old baby, ten-year-old girl and her twelve-year-old brother, their mother and grandparents were living in a leaky shack, in a deserted hamlet, way off the beaten track. The Croatian authorities had threatened to take the two older children away, as they deemed the mother incapable of looking after them. With their mother's blessing, Sara had arranged for the two older children to be looked after at an orphanage and attend school on the coast.

"They have nothing," Sara said. "When you return with the Land Rover, would you be able to bring some warm winter coats for the children, a snowsuit for the toddler and two bicycles please?"

You bet, I thought. It would be great to give these kids something wonderful after what they had been through. My sister and mum sourced the winter clothing from car-boot sales, and I found two used bikes.

The plan to drive the Land Rover for the BRC did not transpire, however I was committed to go. I had the stuff for the children and no work on the immediate horizon, so I decided to go to Knin and surprise the team. I threw a few clothes in a bag, checked the engine oil, filled up with diesel and, in my ten-year-old, high-mileage, red Citroën C15 builder's van, roared off in a cloud of black diesel fumes. I headed towards Newhaven on the south coast to catch the ferry to Boulogne in Northern France. Two hours later, I caught the last ferry at 11 p.m. The crossing was uneventful; the seas were calm with no wind. I slept for the five-hour crossing, curled up in the back of the van. Driving off the ramp, careful not to tear off my exhaust pipe, I was soon out of Boulogne and on my merry way.

I felt great on this crisp sunny day in late October, away on another excellent adventure. This time, Bob Dylan was singing to me via a cassette tape (eight-tracks having gone the way of the dinosaurs). It did seem strange, driving back down through Europe in my little red van. I had become used to travelling around in a highly visible ICRC Land Cruiser with all the protection that came with it.

The three days it took me to transit through Europe and into Croatia passed quickly. I was pulled over just once, after crossing into Croatia. The police gave me a funny look when I explained I was going to Knin to visit some friends; they studied my passport for some minutes but let me go on my way. I followed pretty much the same route I had taken on my bike, as it was the straightest route – probably not the quickest, but the straightest.

I enjoyed recognizing different spots on the way, especially the mountains, and just pressing a little harder on the accelerator pedal instead of pushing a lot harder on the bike pedals. The van ran sweetly with no issues. As a precaution, before I left England, I became a member of the Royal Automobile Club (RAC). For fifteen British pounds extra, in the event of a breakdown, they would guarantee my vehicle recovery from anywhere in Europe. This inexpensive insurance gave me peace of mind on the way back to Knin.

★ ★ ★

During my truck-driving days, breakdowns were a fact of life, as were punctures; we always carried at least one spare wheel. Often on a six-week trip, more than one puncture was the norm; in these circumstances, it became necessary to use one or more of the double trailer wheels to give you four extra chances to keep rolling. If you were unfortunate enough to have even more punctures, the only option was to buy a new or re-treaded tire. But in the Middle East deserts and the mountains of southern Turkey, tire shops were not common. Each trip, I made sure I had one new tire in with the load. Once customs were cleared and the goods delivered, I then had a chance to make some good money selling the extra tire to a desperate truck driver in the middle of the desert.

Every driver treated his clutch, tires and brakes with great care. Mechanical breakdowns were always a challenge, often involving a day-long hitchhiking trip to the nearest town to find a mechanic willing to try to repair the vehicle. This was to be avoided if at all possible as any profit on the trip could easily go to repairs. Most guys doing this kind of trucking were able to nurse an ailing truck into the nearest town and work with the mechanic to keep costs down. A friend of mine had a broken driveshaft in the middle of the Saudi Arabian desert. He had to remove the shaft, then hitchhike

200 kilometres to get it welded, then get back and fit the part before he could continue.

If you had to leave the truck with its load for two days anywhere in Europe, there was a high probability of it being looted or even towed away, never to be seen again. In Saudi Arabia, theft was never a concern: the penalty for theft was to have a hand chopped off, and no thief really wanted that.

I once had a water pump break on a Volvo truck at the bottom of Mont Blanc a week before Christmas. All the repair shops in the area were in holiday mode, so the only option I had was to get a new pump brought out from England with another driver on his way to Iraq. The three days without any heat from the engine were extremely cold. With everything frozen solid, it was quite a challenge fitting the replacement pump.

★ ★ ★

Once more in Knin: late afternoon, with a bit of a chill in the air. Driving into town, I noted that the rubbish piles had grown even more. Clearly, the Croatian authorities needed to get all the rubbish cleared away before a legion of rats took over.

It was the end of the workday, and no one was expecting me. I parked at the delegation, asked where Sara was and headed towards the radio room. Sara had been asking if Zagreb staff had heard any-thing about me arriving with a Land Rover from the BRC, which of course they had not. I stood at the top of the stairs and surprised her. She said it was wonderful for me to bring the stuff for the kids, and my reply was, "I didn't come back for the children, Sara. I came back for you." Her eyes welled with tears, and a smile lit up her face.

Soon we were back at the residence, catching up with all that had happened since I had been gone. Emma, Tommy and Claire arrived soon after; we had a wonderful evening cooking, chatting and drink-ing the odd glass of wine late into the night. Halfway through the evening, Emma told Sara she could take the next day off and visit the three children, so we planned a picnic. We were still pretty sure no one was aware of our affair. The team thought I had returned to see all of them, which of course, in a way, I had. Emma asked me if I'd like to stay upstairs in her spare bedroom; Tommy had moved down with Sara and Claire. I thanked her, but I said the couch in the living room was just fine.

Up early, Sara, her field officer Ana and I loaded the Cruiser with the two bicycles, the snowsuit, two winter coats, boots and clothes. At one of the now-open stores, we stopped to pick up some cheese, Coke and fresh bread, not forgetting the thin, tasty crisps in a cardboard tube. These few items would be a real feast for this family. I loved sitting in the back of the Cruiser, seeing what had changed since I'd left and chatting to Sara and Ana. I noted that there were nowhere near as many soldiers wandering around, no houses and farms burning and many more people in each place we passed through.

As we turned off the main road on the well-worn track towards the hamlet, I didn't think I would be surprised when I actually set eyes on the place. But the two-room hovel was pathetic: patched tin roof, plastic over the windows and old tarps nailed on the outside walls to keep out the wind and rain. The bare earth floors and a smoky open fire burning at one end of the dwelling further shocked me. This unfortunate family had never known anything other than what they now had.

Because of their hard lives, the grandparents appeared to be in their eighties but were most likely in their sixties. The mother was of course much younger. Growing up in the village, she had been treated like an imbecile because she could not speak, which was of course due to her being born mute. She was apparently the hamlet prostitute, and all three children had different, and absent, fathers. She was quite lovely and seemed to accept her lot in life.

As soon as we'd turned off the Cruiser, the girl and boy came charging out of the door, so happy to see Sara and Ana again. Their mother held the baby, followed by the grandparents. We soon headed off to the nearby riverbank for the picnic, where we solemnly washed our hands before sitting down to the feast, which was rapidly devoured, followed by lots of burping as the two-litre bottle of Coke was passed around. The kids and adults were quite content to spend the rest of the afternoon in the sun, talking.

I asked the boy to come and help me with something in the back of the Cruiser. The bikes were covered by a blanket, and his face was a picture of happiness when he saw them. He and his sister held them proudly, posing for a family photo. The mother accepted the winter coats with great dignity.

The 'bicycle' picnic, 1995

Sara explained to their mother the date the two older children would be leaving for the orphanage; she was happy to know they would go to school and receive health care. We promised to visit them when we could. Later that week, Sara and Ana took the children to the orphanage and also visited them once again in late December to find that the children were thriving.

★ ★ ★

Five years later, after finishing a eighteen-month ICRC mission in Georgia: Sara was a medical delegate working in the tuberculosis control program in the penitentiary system; I worked with refugees from the conflict in Chechnya, and Abkhazian IDPs; and Sophie, our three-year-old daughter, attended pre-school in Tbilisi, busily soaking up two languages, Russian and Georgian; we took a two-month trip through Europe, heading home to Canada in our fairly new Russian Jeep, a Lada NIVA. The first leg of our trip took us through Georgia, Turkey, Greece, to Italy via ferry, and via ferry from Italy into Croatia, where after visiting Knin, we stopped and spent an afternoon at the orphanage with the two youngest children. The little boy had joined his big sister and their older brother had finished school and left the orphanage to work. The staff were very professional and caring. The five years had changed the children's lives: they were educated, in good health, and had social skills and a future.

★ ★ ★

I spent the next month in Knin as a volunteer, doing the same work I had done before. Tommy and I responded to requests from the Croatian Red Cross staff; we moved ill and infirm people from remote villages to the new old folks home located in the Knin hospital. We did home repairs to improve safety, taught the Croatian Red Cross staff how to safely drive the Red Cross vehicles and provided support where needed. Many Croatian Red Cross staff were taking over the recovery programs, so the workload was a fraction of what it had been at the height of Operation Storm. Instead of working eighteen-hour days, Tommy and I would often sneak off early to cook dinner for our team. We spent the colder evenings in the kitchen around the stove, eating, talking and just relaxing.

Stanko, who had fled with his family at the start of Oluja, had a brother, Milan, living in Toronto, Canada. Milan made the long journey to Knin to visit his mother, who still lived downstairs. He came to collect some of Stanko's family's belongings and take them to the refugee camp in Serbia, where they had been living since fleeing Knin.

Snow was starting to settle on the mountains; it was time for me to leave. My van was not suited for winter conditions, so when Milan asked if I would take him and his bags to the main bus station in Zagreb, I agreed.

Once more, Sara and I said goodbye. We looked forward to meeting soon in London, at her end of mission, before she went home to Vancouver.

Early morning, with Milan and four large, heavy bags of clothing, we left in another cloud of black smoke. Our journey went up and over the Dinaric Alps to Zagreb. My van's small four-cylinder diesel engine found the going tough. Despite ice and snow on the road, our extra weight gave us enough traction to keep rolling. I closely watched the temperature gauge and the oil warning light. The last thing I wanted was to break down halfway up a mountain. *Would the RAC actually come all the way from the UK to tow me the 1,900 kilometres home?* At the top of the incline, a couple of Zagreb-registered trucks had pulled over to put on snow chains for the slow trip down the mountain; a reminder of my convoyer days in Bosnia.

With a fully loaded truck, slow is the only way to descend any hill or mountain. Even with eighteen wheels and eighteen sets of brake drums and shoes, brakes alone are not enough to get the truck to the bottom safely. Each time the brakes are applied, the drums get hotter and hotter, eventually expanding away from the brake shoes. When the shoes are unable to contact and press against the drums, almost before you know it, you are in trouble. It's frightening when the truck gains speed at an alarming rate, especially when there many more hairpin bends to negotiate.

★   ★   ★

Twenty years previously, on one of my first trips to Iraq, I met up with two English drivers, Ben and Steve, in a truck stop called the Londra Mocamp, just outside Istanbul. Like me, they were resting for a couple of days before starting the arduous second half of the outward trip. Ben and Steve pulled out and left three hours before I did. We had arranged to meet at the British Embassy Club in the capital Ankara two days later and have a beer.

The following afternoon, after slowly and without drama descending a nine-kilometre mountain road, I noticed a Turkish military Jeep parked on the side of a tight turn almost at the bottom of the mountain. A body lay in the back of the Jeep. Looking down the scree slope, I noticed a totally wrecked truck with its load scattered everywhere. Those were Wild-West days in southern Turkey, especially in the wintertime. Then I saw Steve at the bottom, pulled over and sobbing. The body was Ben's, killed when he ran out of brakes. The Turkish soldiers had pulled him out of the wreckage and suggested that Steve go to the British Embassy and report his partner's death.

Most trucks have an exhaust brake, which works by closing off the exhaust pipe, creating back pressure in the engine, enabling the engine to be used as a brake, totally independent of the main brakes. With the correct low gear, it is possible to descend any mountain using the exhaust brake and just occasionally the main brakes. Sadly, it seemed that Ben had got it wrong.

One day later, Steve and I were back at the crash scene, guarding the load Ben had been carrying on his way to Teheran. We had to wait until the embassy could arrange to have a local salvage crew come and recover what they could. Ben's load had consisted of Austin engine parts, cylinder blocks, pistons, big end shells, wheel and engine bearings and carburettor spares. A valuable load. We waited there a week; each night, the temperature dropped to minus twenty degrees Celsius. To keep the propane stove from freezing overnight, I slept with it in my sleeping bag – not the best bed mate.

Even after all these years, I regularly have nightmares in which my brakes have failed, and the thirty-two-tonne truck I'm driving goes faster and faster, no matter how hard I push on the brake pedal.

★   ★   ★

I knew the two Zagreb truck drivers would be going down the mountain slowly. I asked Milan if he minded if we popped into the sub-delegation in Vojnić to check in on the whereabouts of the staff I'd known over the last year.

"Fine, as long as we get to the Zagreb bus station before nine tonight, please," he replied.

Karlovac – front lines between the Republika Hrvatska and the Republic of Serbian Krajina, 1994

The ICRC Vojnić offices had suffered during Oluja; bullet holes and shrapnel damage showed on the outside, in contrast to our offices in Knin, where we had windows and doors blown in, but no bullet holes. The head of sub-delegation was cool towards me and made it clear that I was unwelcome. He was tight-lipped regarding my inquiry about the original staff; all the while I was remembering the "we like you Roger" salami sandwiches. Looking at the damage to the building, it seemed like something very unpleasant occurred there at the height of the battle. I doubt that I'll ever know what happened, and perhaps I don't need to know.

Thirty minutes later, we were back on the road and soon at Karlovac. Framed by four rivers – the Kupa, Korana, Dobra and Mrežnica – the town was built by Austrians in 1579 to defend against the Ottoman Empire. During the Croatian War, the southern part was on the front lines between Republika Srpska Krajina and the Republika Hrvatska and suffered constant shelling that devastated many neighbourhoods, including the area of Turanj where the Croatians had a checkpoint. Two kilometres up the road, the Serbs also had a checkpoint. Many times, on convoy into the Krajinas, I had passed this checkpoint and the Croatian paramilitary police in their distinctive dark blue camouflage uniforms. They took many hours to process our meticulously prepared documents, pushing long, pointed steel rods through every inch of the truckload of food parcels. Supposedly, they were looking for weapons, but in truth, they purposely ruined fifty percent of the load when the rods punctured the one litre can of cooking oil each parcel contained.

Leaving the ruins of Karlovac behind, we soon merged with traffic travelling on the main E65 highway. The toll road and motorway were well maintained. I always felt that I was in modern Europe on this road, especially approaching the glass-fronted capital of Zagreb.

With Milan calling out directions, we were soon at the main bus terminal. The bus to Serbia was fast filling up with people visiting relatives displaced over the last four years. Each passenger appeared to have as many bags as Milan did. All made several relays to load their belongings into the open cargo doors on both sides of the crammed bus. The driver looked like a slightly crumpled, cigarette-ash-dusted, failed airline pilot; epaulettes and gold-braid cap included. He was clearly not going to help with the loading.

"Say hello to Stanko and his family," I shouted as Milan climbed aboard. The start of any journey in the former Yugoslavia was always accompanied by a cloud of smoke. Off they went on the arduous twelve-hour trip to Belgrade.

Fuelled with Croatian diesel, less expensive than elsewhere in Europe, I wanted to cover as many miles as possible before falling asleep at the wheel. The first night I slept for three hours; the second night, I slept for five hours, both in the back of the freezing van. Two days later, I pulled up in front of my sister's house, stumbled upstairs, crawled into bed and slept for fifteen hours.

When I woke up, I called my mate Andy and asked him if he had any work for me for the next week. "Yes. Come up to the barn at Rendcombe," he said.

Two weeks later, and twenty-two months after we first started the conversion, the barn was ready for the owner to move in. I loved laying the beautiful, yellow-grey Cotswold stone. As we finished the project high on top of the Cotswold hills, I looked across the peaceful rolling countryside and saw solidly built, stone-roofed 200-year-old cottages tucked away behind Beech tree windbreaks. I took a long deep breath and, probably for the first time, realized that this was where I belonged.

The gentle English wind and rain felt good on my face.

Buckingham Palace

＊ ＊ ＊ ＊ ＊

November 14, 1995

I was in the front room, watching TV and feeling bored. Still four weeks until Sara would arrive in London for a few days, and then we'd go to Swindon for Christmas. The phone rang, asking for Roger Fowler. Someone claiming to be from the British Red Cross asked, "Would you like to go to Buckingham Palace and meet the Queen?" Surely, this was some kind of joke dreamed up by my friends. "No, this is not a joke," the voice on the telephone assured me. "You have been invited to attend a reception for humanitarian aid workers at six in the evening on November 28th."

"Yes," I said, collecting myself. "I would like to go to Buckingham Palace and meet the Queen."

"That's wonderful. We will send out the invitation today."

Really? I still thought it was a joke, except none of my friends spoke with that kind of well-modulated accent. I have never lived in Cornwall, but I am regularly told that my accent is Cornish. Quite how this developed, I don't know; every one of my friends spoke with a Wiltshire brogue, a kind of middle-England, pastoral muttering, liberally sprinkled with pirate-type words not heard since the Roman Empire decided to give up on this foggy, damp land and return to warm, sunny Italy.

During my time with the ICRC, working with nationalities whose first language was not English, I was careful to utter clear sounds as close to English as possible. This resulted in much head-nodding and gentle smiles, causing a lot less confusion during conversations, but still leaving everyone involved puzzled as to what was actually said. Politicians and diplomats are very good at this. Maria, our Swiss-German Head of Delegation in Split had said more than once during meetings, "Roger! Speak English!"

I headed to the pub to run this latest development past my well-travelled associates. After an hour or two, we concluded that I had received a genuine invitation from the Queen; I should get dressed up and attend.

Walking home that night, I worried about what I should wear. The next morning, the postman delivered an envelope with my name on it, written with what looked like a fountain pen; inside was another envelope containing the actual invitation with my name again written with a fountain pen. And to top it all off, it had a gold-embossed Buckingham Palace stamp.

I knew then this was the real thing. *Who uses a fountain pen anymore?* Written on the bottom of the card was *Dress – Lounge Suit.* Looking through my wardrobe, I realized I had no lounge suit. What *was* a lounge suit anyway? I did have a suit at Mum's that I wore for weddings and funerals. Phoning Mum, I asked if my suit was still in Dad's wardrobe. "Yes, it is."

At my parents' house, I studied the suit, trying to discover a label that said, "Lounge Suit". I found nothing, just the maker's name. It still fitted nicely, so I'd just pretend it was a lounge suit. I could probably borrow Dad's dress shoes if they were not too big. I figured I would not be walking far anyway. The only article of clothing I would need to buy was a new shirt. Mum looked at me, "Has someone died?"

"Oh no," I said. "I'm going to Buckingham Palace to meet the Queen."

Dad looked up from his book and nodded. Mum said, "That'll be nice." Their enthusiasm was palpable. Five minutes later, Dad folded the corner of the page he was on, looked across at me over his reading glasses and said, "Where did you say you were going?"

"Buckingham Palace, Dad."

"Hmm, would you like to borrow my shoes?"

November 28th

The big day. The drive from Swindon along the M4 motorway into London can, depending on the time of day, take anywhere between two and three hours. Being the sort of guy who hates being late for anything, I decided to leave home at one o'clock to leave plenty of time for any hold-ups.

During the last few days, I had been slowly but surely becoming more nervous as the hours ticked away. I phoned the Red Cross offices to speak to the person in charge of the reception; was there any way I could get a parking pass near the palace? It is very difficult to find parking in the city; pay parking fills up quickly and, even if I did want to pay thirty pounds for a few hours parking, it would probably be well outside the city centre involving a bus or tube ride in. Distance would not be ideal, as Dad's shoes were a bit big for any amount of walking. But joy: a parking pass was available. "I'll send it out to you immediately," said the person on the phone. Sure enough, the next day's mail contained the promised parking pass with my name on it and another gold-embossed Buckingham Palace stamp.

I had my suit, shirt and shoes carefully wrapped and hanging in the back of the van. I had filled it with diesel the previous day as a precaution; I didn't want to meet the Queen smelling of diesel. The trip along the motorway went smoothly – not too much traffic, no accidents. As planned, I had hours to spare, so I decided to find the palace parking, then go and kill the remaining time drinking tea in a café somewhere to calm my nerves.

At the front of the palace, there are two main entrances with the police security offices just inside. Hordes of tourists milled about from dawn to dusk, hoping to catch a glimpse of someone famous. (I suspected the royals had several ways to go in and out, other than the main gates.) As I pulled up to the gate and wound down my window, tourists with cameras flashing rushed over and crowded around my not-very-clean van. Blinded by camera flashes, I heard a voice, "Good afternoon, sir. May I help you?"

I explained to the policeman that I was here to meet the Queen, and would he show me where to park, please. The tourists had backed off by now; clearly, I was someone of great importance. Who else would be trying to gain access into Buckingham Palace disguised in an old builder's van? With a humorous look, he said, "Sorry sir, one is unable to visit the Queen today."

To clarify that I was not a lunatic in a red van, I handed him my parking pass. With a look of, *I'll be glad when my shift is over and I won't have to deal with any more goofs today asking to meet the Queen,* he took the pass and went into the security office; I presumed to check the authenticity of the document. The tourists had by this time backed off another few feet but were poised, ready at a moment's notice to rush the vehicle for autographs, souvenirs, hair, bits of clothing, should the driver actually be a celebrity popping in for a cup of tea and a biscuit with Her Majesty. A few moments later, the policeman returned and handed back my pass. I was two hours early for the event. "Sir, would you please return at five thirty this afternoon?" The mass of tourists now gathering and closing in seemed a little deflated when I reversed and roared away.

I found a spot to wait in the van until the desired time. I had ample time to get dressed and tidied up.

I wished I had cleaned out the back of the van. Getting undressed was hard enough but putting on clean clothes amongst the dirt and dust was not easy. I did wonder what might happen if the police had knocked on the window, peered in and saw a semi-naked man, claiming to have an audience with the Queen.

Wearing Dad's shoes, a new shirt and tie and my lounge suit, I arrived back at the security gate. The tourists had thinned out somewhat by this time. A different policeman came over and asked if he could help. Once again, I handed over my now slightly grubby parking pass, which of course I had stepped on while getting changed in the van.

"I won't be a moment, sir," he said and disappeared into the security office. The office windows were darkened, so you could not see what was going on inside. But I imagined six policemen were all looking out at this bloke in a red van, who had what seemed to be a genuine parking pass. Should they arrest him or let him in to see the Queen? With no more ado, I was directed to drive across to the front of the palace. The raked gravel crunched beneath my well-worn tires. I thought of all the royals and world dignitaries who had driven on the same ground, and all the Guardsmen's highly polished boots stamping out a tattoo at the changing of the guard.

The small inner courtyard was surrounded by the Queen's private rooms, some windows with heavy, ornate drapes drawn, and some with chandeliers twinkling, throwing wonderful shadows over the elaborately carved and painted Baroque ceilings. I expected to see a liveried parking attendant directing me into the secure, bomb, gas and nuclear-proof underground parking shelter. But no, just six other cars were parked in a row on the well-raked gravel in the centre. There was a space into which I reversed and turned off the engine. Thinking this spot should be secure, I decided to leave the keys in the ignition. After all, I didn't want to ruin the cut of my Saville Row Gentleman's lounge suit. The camera I had in my pocket produced a small but discrete bulge; that was enough without a bunch of keys in the other pocket.

Ahead I saw a grand portico entrance with lights blazing. At the door, I looked back at the vehicles. There were two Bentleys, two Rolls-Royces, what looked like two Aston Martins – and my red van.

My invitation card said, *No Photographs*, but what the heck, I was prepared, just in case. Just as I was going to take a photo of my van nicely parked in amongst this motoring finery (for the lads' entertainment back at the pub), I noticed a shadow appear. It was cast by a large, immaculately turned out, kilted Highland Guardsman; he travelled complete with silver-handled dirk tucked into his neatly ironed tartan socks. I marched through the door indicated by the soldier and held open by two liveried pages. Handing over my invitation, I thought, *This guy probably has a whole sheep for breakfast, so leave camera in pocket, Roger.* He looked at my invitation and said, "Good evening, Mr. Fowler. Please wait in the anteroom. The reception will commence shortly." *What's an anteroom?* I thought, *A room that's not a room?*

Still not sure if this was actually happening, I wandered off the way he pointed. The anteroom was just through the set of French doors at the other end of the lobby. I'd almost made it when he again appeared silently at my side. I'm thinking, *This is where I get the pat-down, the camera is discovered and I'm asked to leave. Quickly and with no fuss, I would be escorted off the palace grounds by two middle-aged, special branch royal protection officers who are trained to kill politely and painlessly. Thrown out through a small non-descript solid oak door,*

I'd be at the mercy of the footpads, thieves and body snatchers who haunt
the dark, dirty, lawless city streets surrounding the palace.

Happily, this was not the case. He simply knelt and brushed
some dried mud off the bottom of my trouser leg, most probably
picked up from the floor of my van. He then took another look
at me, reached around my neck and straightened the collar of my
lounge suit, then patted me on the shoulder before turning smartly
to attend to the other guests.

Entering the quickly filling anteroom, I found a place to stand
and wait until we were invited to enter through another set of beautiful oak with polished brass French doors into the reception area
proper. At exactly 6 p.m., the final set of French doors swung open
silently on well-oiled hinges to reveal a magnificent, glittering reception room. Her Majesty the Queen stood on a slightly raised area,
with His Royal Highness the Duke of Edinburgh on her right and
Princess Anne on her father's right. They waited to welcome each
of us.

There seemed to be no more than 100 people in attendance.
Everyone quietly lined up to shake the royals' hands. My right hand
was firmly jammed in my pocket in a hopeless attempt to dry off the
sweat that by now was pooling in my palms.

Shaking my rather damp hand, the Queen looked right at me
and said, "Welcome to Buckingham Palace." I had no idea how to
respond, so I gave a little bow and, sounding like a well-dressed
Wiltshire Billy goat, said, "Maaam." I then shook the Duke's hand
and lastly, Princess Anne's.

By this time, the guests had formed little groups, standing and
chatting easily. The uniformed palace staff moved among us, white-
gloved, with drinks balanced on silver trays.

A group of about six male guests stood off to one side. That
looked safe. I made my way over and attached myself to them.
Sipping my gin and tonic from the Waterford crystal ER-etched

glass, I considered taking one for a souvenir; the thought of getting wrestled to the ground by the Highland Guardsman stopped me.

Just as I was thinking this was rather fun and beginning to relax a little, the Duke himself walked over with his equerry and began speaking with my group.

"Good evening, sir. What organization are you with?" he asked the fellow opposite me. There were diplomats and surgeons in the group. *Oh my God, it's my turn.* With his bushy eyebrows slightly lowered and his eyes looking deep into my soul, Prince Philip, Duke of Edinburgh, husband of the Queen, Royal Knight of the Garter, Admiral of the Fleet, Field Marshall and Marshall of the Royal Air Force asked me the same question. "And who are you with, and what do you do, sir?"

"I am a humanitarian relief convoyer and truck driver working for the British Red Cross in the former Yugoslavia, sir."

The Duke appeared to be genuinely interested and asked me a few more questions about my work, then moved on to chat with another group of guests.

At nine I decided to leave and start the drive back to Swindon. Giving a nod to my friend the Highland Guardsman, I headed out, climbed into my van, drove through the still-busy, wet streets of London and picked up the M4 motorway on toward the West Country and Swindon. I might make it to the pub before closing.

ACKNOWLEDGEMENTS

With deepest respect, I thank the International Committee of the Red Cross and the British Red Cross for giving me the privilege to work with the largest humanitarian organization in the world: The International Red Cross and Red Crescent Movement.

With thanks to the ICRC Knin and Split Teams for their friendship and trust.

With thanks to Carmen Berger for her stellar leadership and calm; Lorence Ansermet for her energy and humour; and Jimmy Wilson for being in the right place at the right time.

With special thanks to the people of the former Yugoslavia, good and bad, for allowing me to be a small part of the cataclysmic events that overtook their beautiful country.

With thanks to Sam Schwisberg and Lorimer Shenher for their guidance in getting my book to print.

With thanks to Donna Atmore, Dave Owens and Lynn Van Luven for their editorial eyes; and to Johnny Forbes for his interest and photos.

With thanks to the team at FriesenPress for guiding my memoir to publication.

Heartfelt thanks to my children – Jonathan, Alan and Sophie – for their support and making me realize I should never be left at a computer unsupervised.

Lastly, loving thanks to my wife, Sara, for her patience and quiet understanding.

The Seven Fundamental Principles of the International Red Cross and Red Crescent Movement[4]

Humanity

The International Red Cross and Red Crescent Movement, born of a desire to bring assistance without discrimination to the wounded on the battlefield, endeavours, in its international and national capacity, to prevent and alleviate human suffering wherever it may be found. Its purpose is to protect life and health and to ensure respect for the human being. It promotes mutual understanding, friendship, co-operation and lasting peace amongst all peoples.

Impartiality

It makes no discrimination as to nationality, race, religious beliefs, class or political opinions. It endeavours to relieve the suffering of individuals, being guided solely by their needs, and to give priority to the most urgent cases of distress.

---

4   https://www.icrc.org/en/publication/4046-fundamental-principles
     -international-red-cross-and-red-crescent-movement

Neutrality

In order to enjoy the confidence of all, the Movement may not take sides in hostilities or engage at any time in controversies of a political, racial, religious or ideological nature.

Independence

The Movement is independent. The National Societies, while auxiliaries in the humanitarian services of their governments and subject to the laws of their respective countries, must always maintain their autonomy so that they may be able at all times to act in accordance with the principals of the Movement.

Voluntary Service

It is a voluntary relief movement not prompted in any manner by desire for gain.

Unity

There can only be one Red Cross or one Red Crescent Society in any one country. It must be open to all. It must carry on its humanitarian work throughout its territory.

Universality

The International Red Cross and Red Crescent Movement, in which all societies have equal status and share equal responsibilities and duties in helping each other, is worldwide.

GLOSSARY

* * * * *

APC:	Armoured personnel carrier
ARSK:	Army of the Republika Srpska Krajina (Serbian Army of Krajina) *(Srpska vojska Krajine)*
AK-47:	Ubiquitous assault rifle, thirty-round magazine, 7.62-mm round
ARBiH:	Army of the Republic of Bosnia and Herzegovina *(Armija Republike Bosne i Hercegovine)*
BRC:	British Red Cross
BSA:	Bosnian Serb Army
Canbat:	UN Canadian Battalion
Convoy Leader:	The first truck in a convoy (behind the convoyer)
Convoyer:	The person who conducts and escorts a convoy
Expat:	Expatriate staff (or residents) as compared to local staff/residents
HF:	High Frequency Radio
HMG:	Heavy machine gun

HVO:	Croatian Defence Council *(Hrvatsko vijeće obrane)*, the main force of the Bosnian Croats
IDP:	Internally displaced person who has not crossed an international border to find safety
ICRC:	International Committee of the Red Cross
IED:	Improvised explosive device
JNA:	Yugoslav National Army *(Jugoslovenska narodna armija)*
LMG:	Light machine gun
MAN:	Maschinenfabrik Augsburg-Nürnberg: a cargo truck made in Germany
MASH:	Mobile Army Surgical Hospital
NGO:	Non-governmental organization
POWs:	Prisoners of war
PX:	Post exchange
RAC:	Royal Automobile Club of Great Britain
Rakia:	A fruit brandy native to the Balkans; most popular variation *"sljivovica"*
Republika Hrvatska:	Republic of Croatia
RPG:	Rocket Propelled Grenade
Sitrep:	Situation report
T-55:	Soviet main battle tank, 36-tonnes, four-man crew, deployed in 1949

T-34:	Soviet medium tank, 26-tonnes, three-man crew, deployed in 1940
Tracing Mail:	ICRC Central Tracing Agency, a service to enable detainees and civilians separated by war or natural disaster to restore family contact
UAZ-469:	Soviet military jeep
UNHCR:	United Nations High Commissioner for Refugees
VHF:	Very High Frequency radio

CPSIA information can be obtained
at www.ICGtesting.com
Printed in the USA
BVHW071753250922
647705BV00005B/11/J